Awake Leadership

Awake Leadership

A system for leading with clarity and creativity

by Hilary Jane Grosskopf

AWAKE LEADERSHIP
SOLUTIONS

Contents

Preface i

Introduction 1

Vision 15

Support 47

Structure 63

Tools 91

Context 117

Inspiration 135

Freedom 155

Continuing the Practice 171

Author's Notes 181

Dedicated to Gus, Ryan, and Tiffany.

"Action is movement with intelligence.

The world is filled with movement.

What the world needs is more conscious movement,

more action."

- B.K.S. Iyengar

Preface

Preface to Awake Leadership

There are many different reasons for becoming a leader. Some people work hard to secure a leadership position while others are asked to step up into a leadership role. Everyone's experience as a leader will be completely unique. Beyond just a job, assuming the responsibility of a leader can be a transformational experience. Your experience as a leader will not follow a syllabus like you find in school. That is the cool part. However, inheriting a new role within an organization and leading a team can be overwhelming without the right guidance and encouragement.

I joined the corporate world of retail because I was passionate about the products and learning. I started as an intern, became an analyst after graduating from school, then became a manager and, finally, a leader. I became a leader through a series of pretty organic events, though I did step up and ask to be a leader. Why did I want the experience of leading a team? Being part of a team is fun but teaching, sharing, and creating experiences for people are some things I have always enjoyed since I was young. Having the opportunity to do this in an applied setting where I was enthusiastic about the products and to choose who was helping me was like a dream.

When I became a leader, I realized there isn't a lot of guidance for how to onboard to a new role in an organization and start leading a team. There were many books that detailed qualities of great leaders but I could not find guidance about what successful modern leadership looks like in action. *How do I delegate? How do I make sure we accomplish our objectives? How do I keep the team motivated in a dynamic, often chaotic work environment?* I needed a solution for **how** to lead my team so we could continuously align to achieve our objectives.

I started analyzing my team, our scope of work, and the larger picture of what we needed to achieve to take responsibility of the work. I put a lot of energy into understanding what my responsibilities really were, what the team Vision was, and how to lead the team forward in a way that worked for the organization as well as the team members.

While developing my leadership methodology, I also found that the imbalance of clear direction, creativity, and autonomy within organizations set the stage for failure. Team members often felt they didn't receive enough clear direction, they didn't receive enough autonomy, or they didn't feel a sense of connection to the team and mission.

My objective was to create exercises and rituals for my team that would help us align and accomplish our objectives. I also had to find that sweet spot of clear direction and creative freedom for everyone to feel satisfying progress, individual autonomy, and connection. I drew inspiration from an ancient system that had helped me gain a personal balance of structure and freedom in my own life. By practicing specific exercises with my team, we achieved our objectives and progressed individually and collectively. The day-to-day experience was one of satisfying progress, learning, and connection rather than anxiety and forced progress. In this guidebook, I'll share this essential system and exercises with you.

There are many leadership books and courses out there that offer solutions for more optimal productivity and team building. However, few existing, affordable resources show **how** - *in action* - to lead a team within an organization. This is what I offer to you.

There is a need for Awake leaders; leaders that value clarity, creativity, and genuine connections over forced, empty progress and achievement. Successful leaders of the future will work to find the actions that allow themselves and their team members to progress authentically. I hope you enjoy the guide and that this system serves as a valuable resource for your leadership journey.

xo Hilary

Introduction

The Call for Awake Leaders

Leadership is a buzzword in communities and organizations around the world. As populations, industries, and organizations continue to evolve and grow, leadership has gained even more traction as its own area of study and development. There are many different kinds of leaders out there and the world is calling for stronger, more creative leaders. Many founders, executives, and top-level managers say they are looking for leaders with knowledge, experience, and tools. However, what the world really needs is more Awake Leaders: visionary, responsive, resourceful, enthusiastic leaders. Organizations need leaders that can lead the team and the Vision forward.

What are the qualities of an Awake leader? An Awake leader is enthusiastic about change and people. An Awake leader responds to changes and reaches objectives efficiently and creatively with the team. He or she is clear on the team Vision and maximizes the strengths of the team. An Awake leader displays dedication, driven by curiosity. He or she has a balance of hard and soft skills. An Awake leader is authentically inspirational and influential. He or she enjoys learning, analyzing, and synthesizing. An Awake leader can zoom in to understand detail and zoom out to see the big picture impacts. He or she generates ideas for how to evolve, sustainably solve problems, and supports change and growth in the company through efficient execution. An Awake leader walks the walk and leads by example. An Awake leader cultivates enthusiasm, curiosity, and a culture of collaboration and follow through. An Awake leader has a mindful method to their madness.

Every leader's mission and journey will be completely different. Though it may seem straightforward to be a leader within an organization, it's actually really challenging in practice to both take direction and give direction. It's challenging to cultivate an authentic leadership style and qualities when surrounded by organizational norms and structure. It's challenging to both respond to change and lead change. I have found that a specific set of actions provides a foundation for a successful leadership practice within dynamic organizations, while allowing leaders to cultivate an authentic leadership style and qualities. In this guidebook, you'll learn this essential system for successful leadership in practice.

◆　◆　◆

The Awake Leadership System

The Awake Leadership system is a specific progression of actions for producing results by moving the Vision forward in a way that is engaging. It is a system of actions for leading with a balance of clear structure and creative freedom. Many leaders have a knack for providing direction but the team culture feels like a strict, boring factory day-to-day. Other leaders are chill, fun, and inspiring but the team lacks clear direction and alignment. Both of these situations have strengths but both have weaknesses that can inhibit the ultimate success, wellness, and progress of the team. By leading with a balance of Structure and Freedom, you can meet your objectives with more efficiency and enthusiasm.

I developed the Awake Leadership system during my experience as a team member and leader within a variety of organizations. The system is designed with love for leaders within organizations and small business leaders. Leaders that are starting a new role or new to an organization can use the guide to onboard in just one month and start driving changes within their first quarter. Seasoned leaders can use the guide to learn to reach their objectives with more clarity, efficiency, and ease. The guide is designed for leaders of all ages, and intended to help build bridges between leaders of different generations and backgrounds. The system is meant to enable and encourage diverse teams to work toward collective objectives.

The Awake Leadership system is for leaders seeking to

✔ **Take ownership of responsibilities accomplish objectives with more ease and enthusiasm**

✔ **Balance clear direction with creative freedom**

✔ **Cultivate a team environment full of genuine connection and satisfying progress**

✔ **Learn specific actions for leading the team and Vision forward while cultivating authentic, Awake Leadership qualities**

✔ **Identify strengths and blind spots in order to cultivate a well-rounded leadership practice**

In this guidebook, you will learn and practice new ways of thinking about leadership and you will learn a system for leadings your team's work that is sustainable. You may even begin to realize that aspects of your job that seemed stressful, confusing, or limiting become easier and more enjoyable.

◆ ◆ ◆

The Seven Vitals

The Awake Leadership system addresses seven leadership vitals. These seven vitals cover the spectrum of leadership practices for keeping your team aligned and enthusiastic while working toward the Vision. The vitals are not just leadership qualities or attributes; they are pillars that represents sets of specific **actions** for aligning teams and fueling progress collectively and individually.

Vision

Support

Structure

Tools

Context

Inspiration

Freedom

The seven vitals of Awake Leadership are specific areas or centers for leaders to focus on in order to lead with a balance of clarity and creativity. The first, foundational vital of the Awake Leadership system is Vision. Without an understanding of what the team is responsible for and the ability to communicate this to the team, there is no way to progress together. You'll learn how to develop and articulate your team Vision in the first section. Next, a leader must gather Support for the team. Without the right Support for each team member, the team has no fuel to work toward the Vision. The third vital is Structure. Structure is how the Vision comes to life, through delegation and specific timing of tasks. It aligns your team around how the Vision will be accomplished. The fourth vital is Tools. Tools are extensions of your abilities as a team. You tool belt helps you to work toward your Vision optimally. Next is Context, where we go beyond the realm of your immediate team to understand the larger organization and where your team fits into the big picture. The sixth vital is Inspiration. Inspiration is what keeps the team engaged, motivated, and innovative. Inspiration keeps the Vision alive and fresh. Finally, in the Freedom section, you'll explore what makes you unique as a leader and learn how to foster a balance of Structure and Freedom for yourself and your team.

The vitals serve as focus points or check points for identifying strengths and blind spots. Leaders often have a few of the vitals covered but totally ignore one or more that are, yes, *vital* to the success of the team. Once you work through all seven sections, you'll have an understanding of the vitals. You'll have the ability to identify where your strengths and blind spots are at any given point in time and in any given situation.

◆ ◆ ◆

Working through the Guidebook

The Awake Leadership system is a specific progression of **actions** for leading in order to accomplish your objectives as a team. The guidebook works in order of the seven vitals, from Vision to Freedom. However, the practice is iterative; you will continue to work through the vitals and revisit them as you progress with your team.

Each section begins with an introduction and then provides applied exercises and examples to put the vital into practice. The exercises were developed for teams of two to eight people. However, solo leaders and team members can also benefit from the concepts and from doing the exercises on their own. If you have a team of greater than eight people, consider breaking the team up into groups to do the exercises and then reconvene to discuss as a whole. I suggest that you (the leader) read and try the exercises on your own first before trying them out with your team. Preparation is key and you'll be able to better gauge if a certain exercise is best for your team. I strive to do more showing than telling, so each exercise also contains real examples and explanations from teams in the field. One of my favorite aspects of the exercises is that no technology is required. All the exercises provide a chance to get off the computer and reconnect with your team and with yourself. Finally, each of the seven sections concludes with an Awake Tip, which provides an important insight related to the section content. The Author's Notes in the back of the book contains a suggested schedule for working through the guidebook but please work at your own pace! Allow the concepts to sink in as you apply them in practice and take your time.

◆　　◆　　◆

Let's get started!

The Awake Leadership guide does not require you to buy any fancy software or download any apps. This process is a lot about stripping away complexity. It helps to have a budget for supplies, new tools, and travel but you can be an Awake leader whether you have zero budget or unlimited budget. To be an Awake Leader, you just need dedication to improving, a bit of time to read the guide, and an open mind. Don't get too technical or obsessive about getting it right. In the beginning, it's all about learning to enjoy it. Try out the method and actions from the exercises and see if they work for you. I share them because they worked for my teams. Proceed with the intention of learning and enjoy the journey!

Warm-Up Reflection

Write down brief answers to the following reflection questions. Nothing too fancy. We'll be writing throughout the guide so consider this a warm up!

What do you like about the organization you work for? Why, of all places, do you work there and do this work? Write down anything and everything you love about it. Whatever comes to mind. *The work environment, the perks, the people, the mission, the products or services, the location, the benefits, the discount you get on products and services...*

_____

_____

_____

_____

_____

_____

_____

_____

_____

_____

Who are leaders that you admire? List a few well-known leaders as well as some of your leaders at work or the world at large that you admire. What do you admire about them?

_____

_____

_____

_____

_____

What is your intention as a leader? What kind of leader would you like to be? What do you feel is the most important thing you provide for your organization and for your team?

_____

_____

_____

_____

_____

_____

_____

Let's begin our journey up the spiral staircase of
Awake Leadership.

The Seven Vitals

1

Vision

noun;

the act of being able to see

a manifestation to the senses of something
immaterial

Vision

What is Vision?

Vision is the foundation for Awake Leadership. Before delegating and digging into the work, you must know where you're going as a team. What is the objective? How do you work toward your objectives? What does success look like at the end of a project, the end of a week, or the end of the year? This is what you will clarify in this first section.

What is a visionary leader?

A visionary leader is clear about what his or her team's responsibilities and objectives are. He or she is able to articulate to the team what the Vision is and how the team will work toward it. He or she takes ownership of the team's scope of work to bring the Vision to reality. If you feel like you're lacking in any of these areas now, don't worry or give up. We'll work on this in the exercises.

I meet many leaders that believe visionary leaders are the founders and entrepreneurs with big world-changing ideas. This is true, however, I believe we need visionary leaders within every organization, at every level.

A founder or CEO designs the Vision for the organization. However, if you're a leader within an organization, the Vision is handed down to you by your leader. This is why it's important that top-level leadership is visionary. I do not mean visionary in terms of just having ideas and being inspiring; visionary also means they clearly articulate the Vision to their leadership team. It's then up to the leadership team to be visionary in their own respective realms. Each leader must be able to translate the overall big-picture organizational Vision into what that means for their specific area and team. Without clarity and direction, your team will be going through motions without intention and this approach likely won't lead to successfully reaching your objectives. A clear Vision is essential. A method for communicating the Vision and measuring progress makes showcasing your team's work and contributions a lot easier.

Why is Vision a leadership vital?

Teams that work with a clear collective Vision accomplish objectives successfully, with efficiency and enthusiasm. When the team has the Vision in mind, they see how their individual work contributes to the larger whole. Team members can then better take ownership of their work to meet the larger objective. They work with intention.

In this section, you'll work to answer important questions including, *What is my team's core mission? What are our main responsibilities, priorities, and objectives? What are my key metrics and results that my team and I are evaluated on?* These questions may seem simple. However, I'm always surprised at how many leaders cannot provide straightforward answers to these important questions, even months or years after they step into their leadership role. The answers often get lost in transitions and amongst the day-to-day work over time. If someone like your leader, a family member, or a new acquaintance at a conference asked you these questions, what would you say? Knowing the answers to these questions will help you to focus and to move toward your objectives. Let's begin the exercises.

Vision Exercises

The purpose of the Vision exercises is to clarify and articulate your Team Vision. In the first exercise, you'll make your Role Map to gain clarity about your own expectations, responsibilities, and objectives. In Exercise 2, you'll draft your team's mission statement. Finally, in Exercise 3, you'll chart your Team Vision Map to articulate your Team Vision. The Vision Map will show how your team operates today and what your most important objectives really are. You'll then be able to identify places where you could optimize and organize your scope of work.

Exercise 1: Your Role Map

Exercise 2: Team Mission Statement

Exercise 3: Team Vision Map

Supplies

✎ Pencil or pen
✎ Colored Pencils (optional)

Vision

Exercise 1: Your Role Map

A Role Map is a diagram used to clarify, organize, and show the full scope of your role at any point in time. It's a visual, organized representation of what you contribute to the organization. The Role Map serves four primary purposes.

1 Gain clarity about your position scope and responsibilities

2 Reference during one-on-one meetings with your leader

3 Reference during performance reviews to show progress

4 Facilitate smooth, efficient transitions within the company

Why is a Role Map essential for visionary leaders?

Many leaders inherit or assume new roles without understanding what their objectives, responsibilities, and expectations really are. Taking an honest look at your responsibilities and expectations may sound stressful at first but I have found that, for most leaders, the stress is actually due to the fact that their responsibilities and objectives are unclear or overly complex. Uncertainty around if you're doing and focusing on the right things is distracting. It leads to burnout and lack of productivity. You can't exceed expectations and achieve your bonus without knowing what the expectations are in the first place! We'll work to gain this clarity here.

Role Mapping sets clear expectations for what you should accomplish and contribute toward the overall organizational Vision. Most importantly, you need to have clarity about your own role and responsibilities before you start to think about your team's.

Preview!

Here is an example of a finished Role Map:

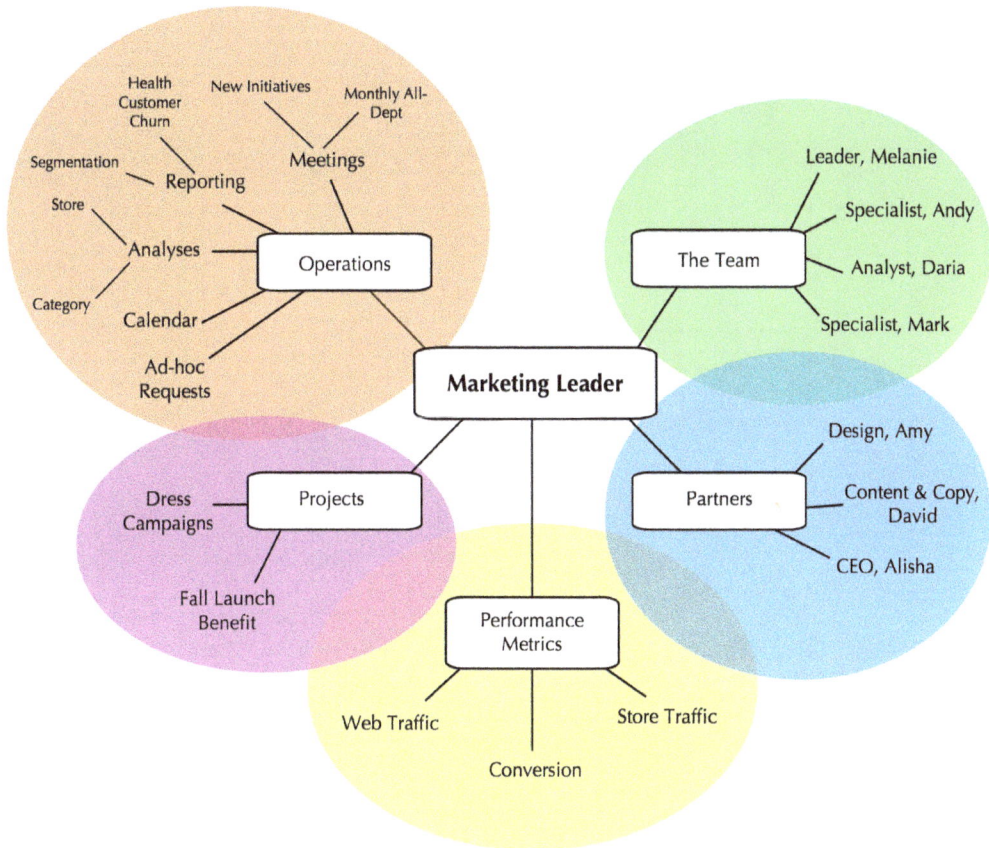

Note: A Role Map is a structured Mind Map. Mind Mapping is a technique that was invented by Tony Buzan. I use Mind Mapping because it is a great visual technique for collaboration as well as personal organizing, understanding, and brainstorming. It's essential for getting information out of your head (or your leader's) and onto paper!

Vision

The Role Map

The central topic of the Role Map is your position title. The first layer of the map contains five specific components that are important for every leader in organizing and clarifying their role: Team, Partners, Operations, Projects, and Performance Metrics.

Here is the **Role Map base** with the first layer of branches:

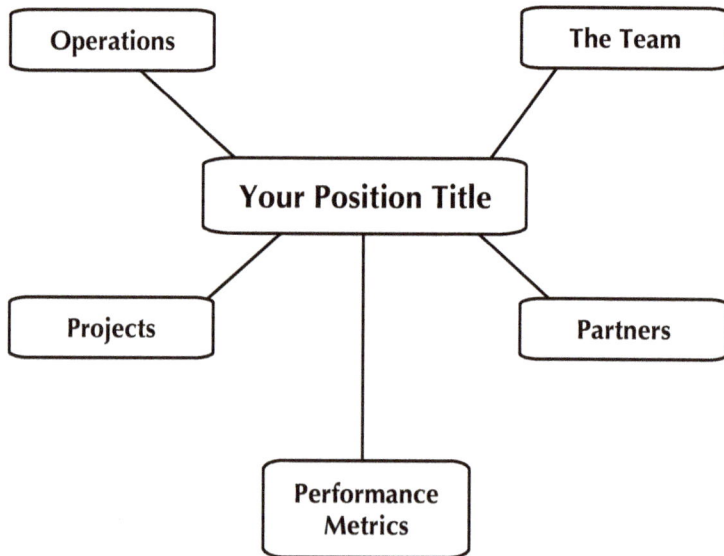

```
   Operations                         The Team


            Your Position Title


   Projects                           Partners


              Performance
                Metrics
```

The First Layer Branches

Read below for the descriptions of the five standard first layer branches of every Role Map.

Team: On the Team branch, you'll add the position names and given names of your team members, including yourself.

Partners: On the Partners branch, you'll continue by adding the position names and given names of your key collaborators. For example, if you're an operations leader, you may collaborate with the quality leader and department. Leaders typically have between three and six key collaborators.

Operations: The Operations branch, you'll detail your ongoing tasks and responsibilities. This is the most complicated branch for most leaders. This is the branch where you will show everything you do day-to-day, week-to-week, month-to-month, etc – everything you do on an ongoing basis.

Projects: The fourth branch is for special projects and initiatives. This branch displays the development projects your team is working on. As opposed to operational tasks, Projects are one-time efforts.

KPIs (Key Performance Indicators or Performance Metrics): What are the key metrics where your impacts – the impact of your role – show through? This can also include qualitative objectives like company morale and engagement of team members. It's important to be able to align with your leader and team as to what signifies all is going well and you're fulfilling the expectations and purpose of your role.

Vision

The Second Layer Branches

Now that we have an understanding of the standard first layer branches of the Role Map, it's time to branch the second layer. Let's use an example to illustrate how to branch off each first-layer component. Refer to the Marketing Leader example on the next page.

Melanie, the leader of Marketing, made her map using the Role Map base.

Team: To begin, she added the members of her team to the map including herself. She has three team members.

Partners: She then added her key collaborators within the organization. She put three key collaborators on the map.

Operations: Melanie identified five operational areas for her team. These are five areas where there are ongoing tasks and activities happening. She then added a second layer to include the specific tasks and activities.

Projects: She then added the team projects. Her team is working on two key projects right now.

KPIs: Finally, she added her team's key performance indicators. Melanie talked with her leader, the CEO, and they agreed that her team's metrics of success in marketing are Web Traffic, Store Traffic, and Conversion Rate.

This is a relatively simple example but the cleaner you can make your map, the more clear your focus points will be.

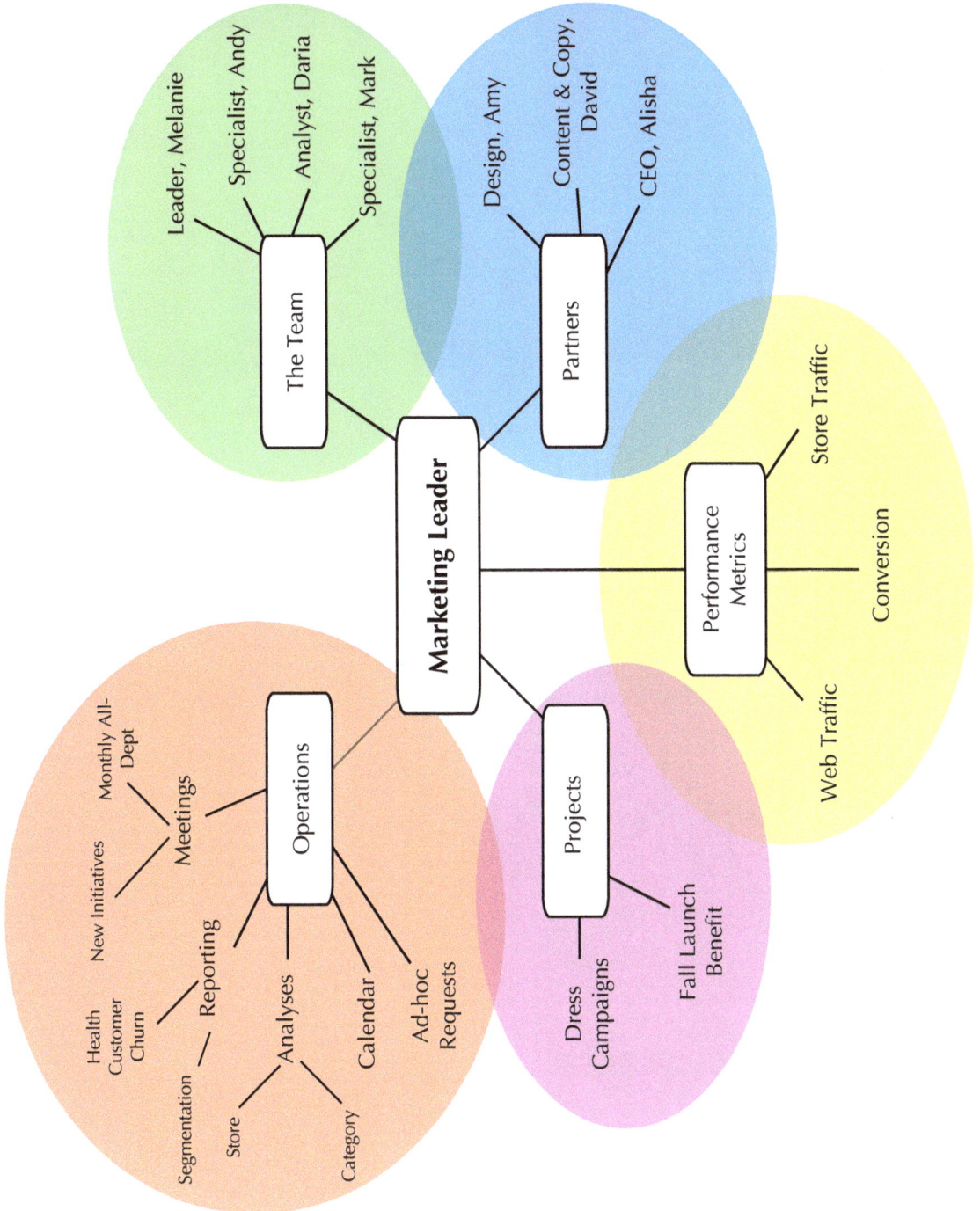

Marketing Leader

The Team
- Leader, Melanie
- Specialist, Andy
- Analyst, Daria
- Specialist, Mark

Partners
- Design, Amy
- Content & Copy, David
- CEO, Alisha

Performance Metrics
- Store Traffic
- Conversion
- Web Traffic

Operations
- Meetings
  - Monthly All-Dept
  - New Initiatives
- Reporting
  - Health
  - Customer Churn
  - Segmentation
- Analyses
  - Store
  - Category
- Calendar
- Ad-hoc Requests

Projects
- Dress Campaigns
- Fall Launch Benefit

Generalized Role Map Example

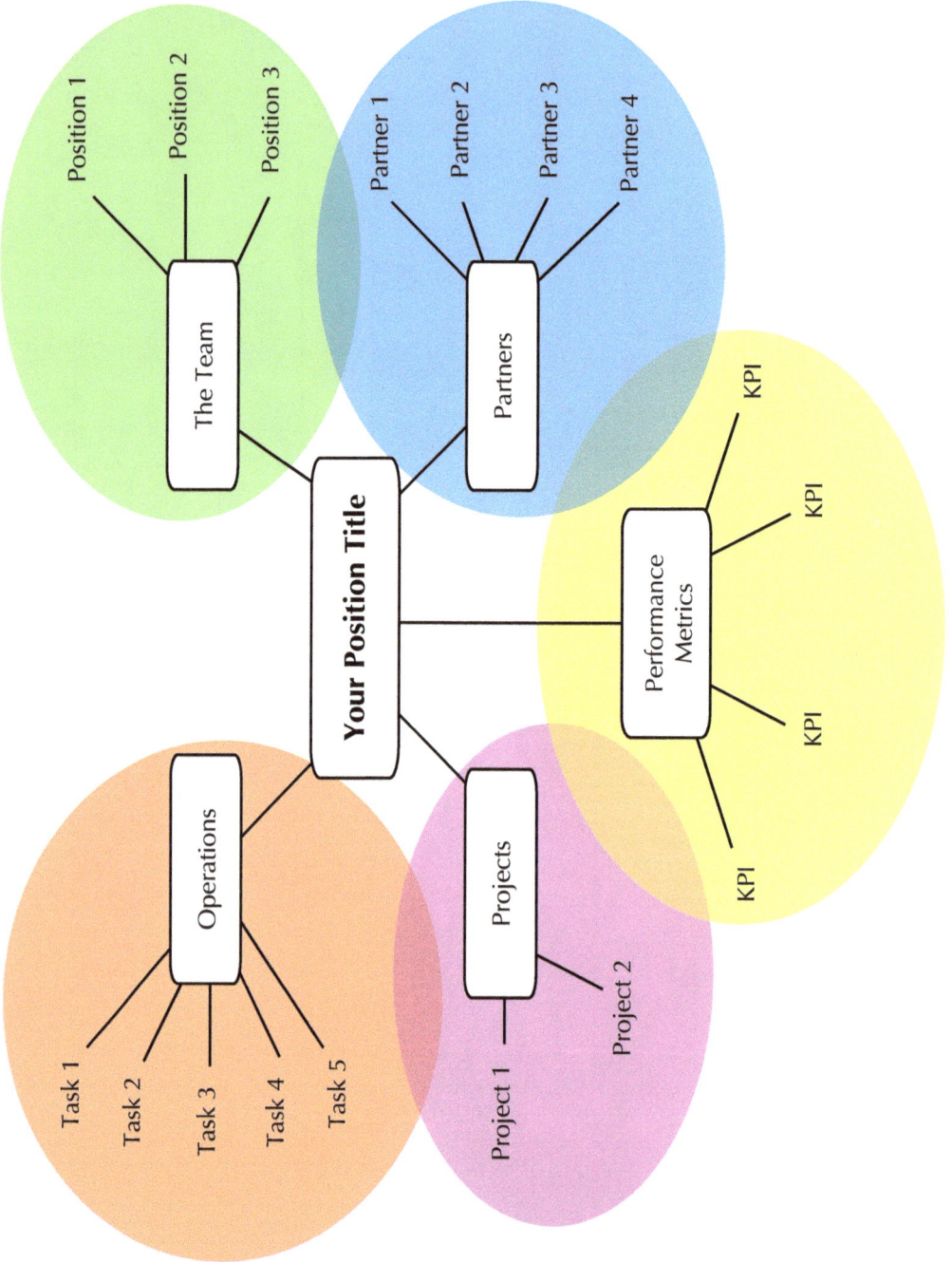

The Team
- Position 1
- Position 2
- Position 3

Partners
- Partner 1
- Partner 2
- Partner 3
- Partner 4

Your Position Title

Performance Metrics
- KPI
- KPI
- KPI
- KPI
- KPI

Operations
- Task 1
- Task 2
- Task 3
- Task 4
- Task 5

Projects
- Project 1
- Project 2

Your Turn!

Use the Role Map base below to draft your Role Map. Begin by placing your position title in the center and then branch to form the second layer, starting with your Team branch. There is additional Role Map paper in the Author's Notes in the back of the book.

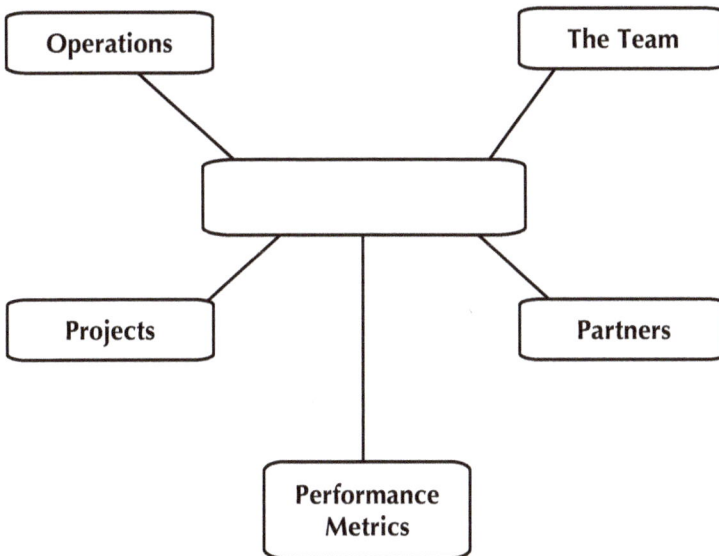

```
   Operations                          The Team


              [                    ]


   Projects                            Partners


                 Performance
                   Metrics
```

<u>Note</u>: You can also use a digital tool like slides or a spreadsheet with shapes to create your Role Map. There are many great online tools for Mind Mapping as well.

Vision

Tips for Making and Using Your Role Map

◆ Remember that this is a new skill to learn and your Role Map will take some time and thought to create. Don't be afraid to ask your leader for help.

◆ A Role Map clarifies your own role and blind spots you may have. Common blind spots are: *What are my metrics for success, really?* and *Who are my key partners in the organization?* among others. Work to clarify the answers.

◆ The Role Map does not only serve as a tool for you to understand and organize, but also as a communication mechanism with your leader. Bring your Role Map to touch bases with your leader to review what you're currently working on and where you need support.

◆ How often should you update your Role Map? It's up to you how often to update your Role Map. I would suggest updating it at least once per month. However, sometimes I would look back at or update mine every week. It's a helpful rock to work from when you have crazy days or weeks. *Are you focusing on the right things? What is changing and needs to change on the map to keep your focus on the right areas?*

◆ Remember that your team and your work will benefit from this clarity. Be patient and persistent as you create your Role Map.

Keep you Role Map accessible. You will need it for future exercises!

Exercise 2: Team Mission Statement

A mission statement is a one-sentence statement that describes what your team contributes to the organization and, ultimately, what you do for the customer, audience, or end-user. The team mission statement is where we begin to transition from thinking on an individual level to a collective, team level.

Why Write a Team Mission Statement?

By writing a mission statement, you'll clarify the true purpose of your team – not just what you do day-to-day but how it impacts the end-user on a human level. You'll clarify **why** you do the actions you have on your Team Vision Map.

It often seems extra to have a mission statement but it's actually an important tool for aligning your team around the Vision. As an organization grows, it's important for leaders to understand and reconnect back to how their team contributes to the larger whole.

Finally, if you ever find that you struggle to tell others like professional contacts, family, or friends what you do and why, this exercise will help to make that statement simple and meaningful. A mission statement can also be used for professional networking.

Vision

The Mission Statement

So, how do we begin? There are many methods for writing a mission statement but I have simplified the Awake Leadership mission statement to consist of just three pieces of information: your team name, your contribution to organization, and the impact on the customer or end-user. If you know these three things, you can write your mission statement. You probably do know these pieces of information but it may not seem so simple or easy to access. We'll work through it here.

Here is the template for writing your mission statement:

The mission of the _____ **team**

is to _____ **in order**

to _____.

Complete the prompts on the next page to prepare to draft your Team Mission Statement. You can refer to the examples on the page following the prompts.

Mission Statement Prompts

1. What is your team name?

_____

2. What do you contribute to your organization? What key actions do you take on behalf of the organization? *Hint: You can pull actions from your Operations branch on your Role Map.*

_____

_____

_____

_____

3. How do you impact the customer or end-user? What is the end-user benefit or impact of the actions you take?

_____

_____

_____

_____

Vision

Mission Statement Examples

Example 1: Retail Store Team

The mission of the Newport Beach Store Team is to provide a seamless in-store experience in order to connect customers with products they love and enhance their connection with the brand.

Example 2: Customer Service Team

The mission of the Customer Service Team is to provide information and resolutions in order to resolve customer concerns and questions, as well as improve the overall customer experience.

Example 3: Logistics Operations Team

The mission of the Logistics Operations Team is to manage, execute, optimize, and troubleshoot operations in order to ensure our customers receive products safely and on time.

Example 4: Marketing Team

The mission of the Marketing Team is to create compelling campaigns and content as well as optimize and manage the ongoing marketing operations in order to increase customer awareness, engagement, and adoption of the brand.

Your Turn!

Use the space below to draft your Mission Statement using the template format and your answers to the three prompts.

_____

_____

_____

_____

_____

_____

_____

_____

_____

Remember to be patient and take time in drafting your statement. Review it with your team and leader for feedback!

Vision

Exercise 3: Team Vision Map

A Team Vision Map is a visual representation of what your team does for the organization in **action**. It shows how your team works toward the mission. A Team Vision Map enables the team to align around objectives and make progress together.

Why is a Vision Map essential?

When the team can align around the Vision, confusion is stripped away. A Team Vision map provides focus and enables collective progress toward expectations and objectives.

The Vision Map serves four primary purposes.

1 Gives team members clarity about the team's current work scope to stay aligned in action

2 Reference during one-on-one meetings with your team members to discuss progress and planning

3 Reference in team meetings to measure and discuss progress collectively

4 Reference during performance reviews to measure and discuss progress

Turn the page to begin making your Team Vision Map!

Vision

The Vision Map

The central topic of the map is your team name. The first layer contains three specific components that are important for every team to align on: Operations, Projects, and Team Building & Development. We'll review each in more detail on the next page. Similar to your Role Map, the second layer will contain your details for each of these three first layer branches.

Here is the Vision Map base with the first layer of branches:

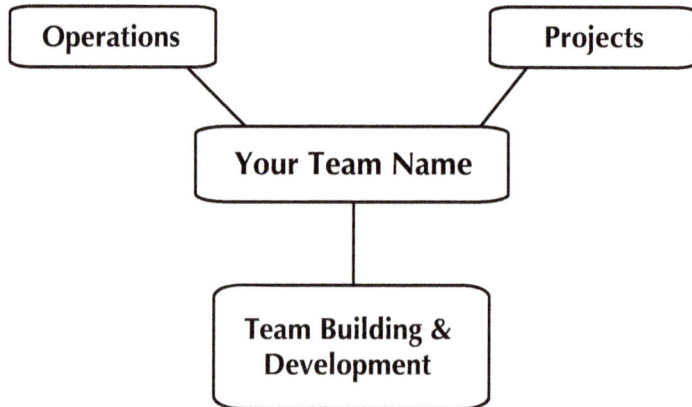

```
┌──────────────┐                    ┌──────────────┐
│  Operations  │                    │   Projects   │
└──────────────┘                    └──────────────┘
          \                          /
           \   ┌────────────────┐   /
            \──│ Your Team Name │──/
               └────────────────┘
                       │
              ┌────────────────┐
              │ Team Building &│
              │  Development   │
              └────────────────┘
```

The First Layer Branches

Read below for the descriptions of the three standard first layer branches of every Team Vision Map.

Operations: Your team Operations branch should largely resemble your Role Map operations tasks and activities. So you can begin by replicating your Role Map Operations branch on your Team Vision Map. As you detail this branch, you may want to work through it with your team members to make sure you have included all the team's ongoing tasks and activities.

Projects: Similarly, the Projects branch on your Team Vision Map should resemble your Role Map's Project branch. You can also replicate your Role Map Projects branch on the Team Vision Map. Consult with your team to make sure you have not missed any projects they are currently working on or planning to begin soon.

Team Building and Development: Finally, a new one! Team Building and Development opportunities are important for team members to feel engaged and to build essential skills and expertise. Since things change so frequently in terms of industry landscape, best practices, and tools, continuous learning is important. Team building activities keep the team human and connected at a deeper level than a transactional, operational unit. Even if you are a remote team, gather together periodically. Use this map as part of your team discussions and activities.

Vision

The Second Layer Branches

Now that we have an understanding of the three components of the Team Vision Map, it is time to branch to make the second layer. Let's use an example to illustrate how to branch off each component. Refer to the Marketing Team example below and follow along with the example on the next page.

Melanie, Leader of Marketing, made her Team Vision Map using the Vision Map base.

Operations: Melanie replicated the Operations branch from her Role Map. She consulted with team members and included everything they do on an ongoing basis.

Projects: She then added the same two projects to the map.

Team Building and Development: Melanie has added the team events and development activities. She added a Team Offsite event, True Metrics Training (a tool they use on their team), Leadership Lunch, and a Department Scavenger Hunt event coming up.

Again, this is a relatively simple example since it is a small team but keeping things simple and clean keeps the focus clear. Include only what is essential! An aligned, focused team makes collective progress efficient and leaves space for more of the exercises coming up in the sections that follow.

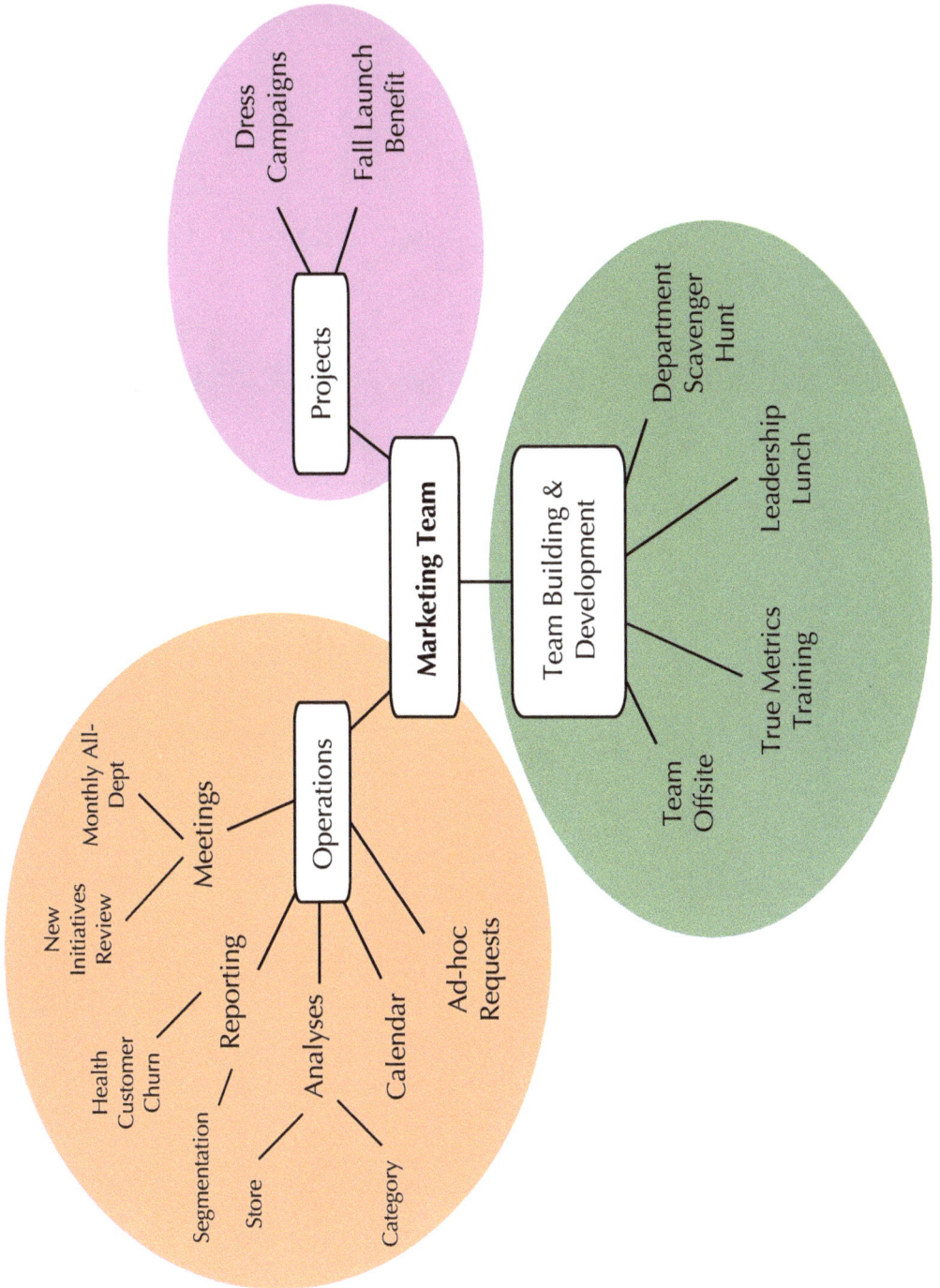

Marketing Team

Projects
- Dress Campaigns
- Fall Launch Benefit

Team Building & Development
- Department Scavenger Hunt
- Leadership Lunch
- True Metrics Training
- Team Offsite

Operations
- Meetings
  - Monthly All-Dept
  - New Initiatives Review
- Reporting
  - Health
  - Customer Churn
- Analyses
  - Segmentation
  - Store
  - Category
- Calendar
- Ad-hoc Requests

Vision

Generalized Vision Map Example

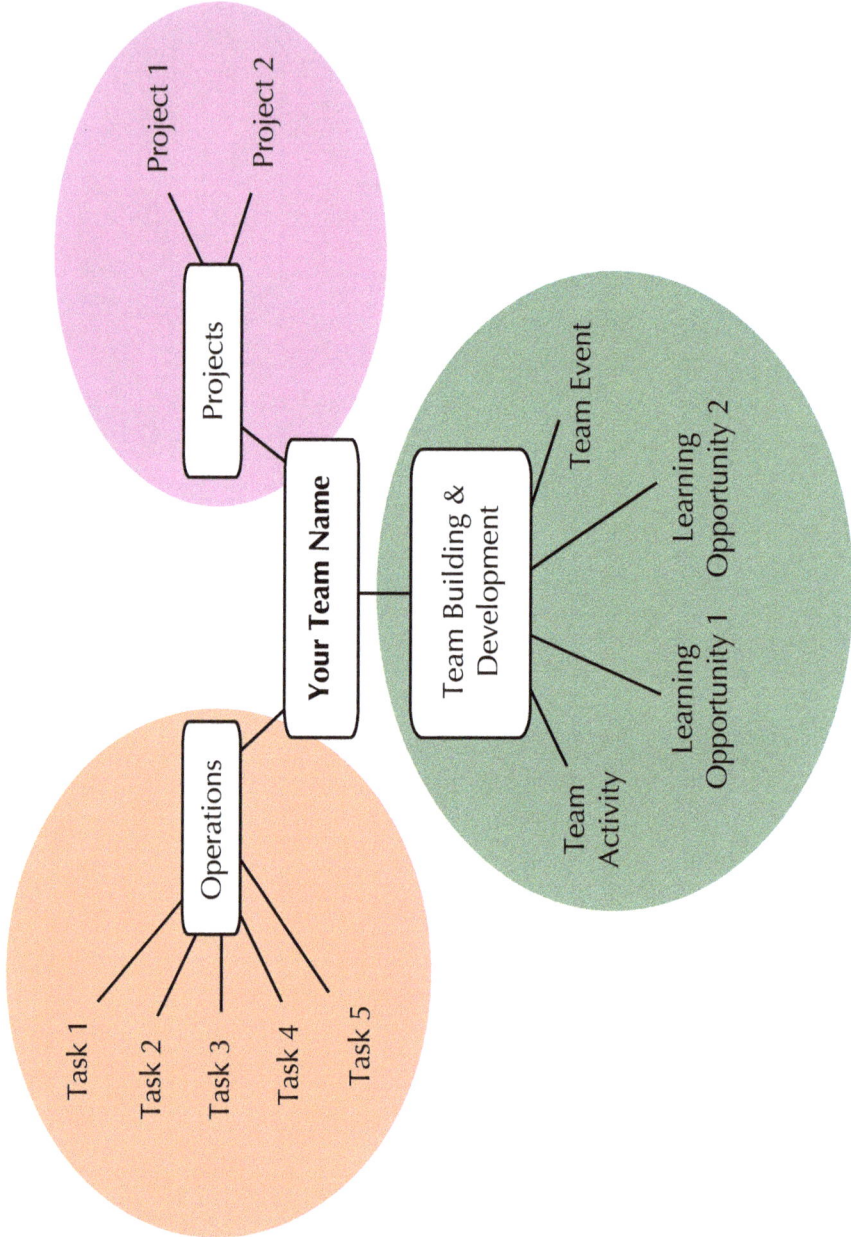

Projects
- Project 1
- Project 2

Your Team Name

Operations
- Task 1
- Task 2
- Task 3
- Task 4
- Task 5

Team Building & Development
- Team Event
- Learning Opportunity 2
- Learning Opportunity 1
- Team Activity

Your Turn!

Use the base below to draft your Team Vision Map. Begin by putting your team name in the center and then begin branching, starting with the Operations branch. There is additional Team Vision Map paper in the Author's Notes in the back of the book.

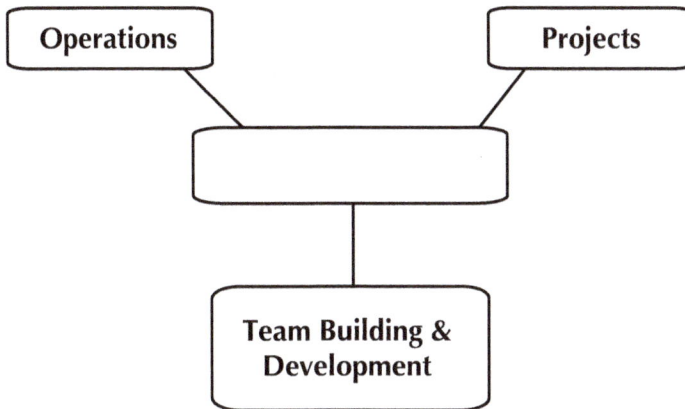

```
┌─────────────┐              ┌─────────────┐
│ Operations  │              │  Projects   │
└─────────────┘              └─────────────┘
          \                    /
           ┌──────────────────────┐
           │                      │
           └──────────────────────┘
                      │
              ┌───────────────┐
              │ Team Building &│
              │  Development   │
              └───────────────┘
```

Vision

Tips for Making and Using your Team Vision Map

◆ Remember that this is a new skill to learn and your Team Vision Map will take some time and thought to create. Like any new process, it can take time to make it feel like a regular team ritual. Put time aside with the team every Monday and/or Friday to review and update the map. It's a good excuse for a team meeting (with snacks)!

◆ Making the Team Vision Map will expose blind spots. I don't mean blind spots in a negative way here but, more specifically, I mean that if you aren't aware of everything your team members do day-to-day, this is a chance to get informed and understand the full-picture scope of work. You should know so that you have clarity about how you're all working toward the Vision. You can then work from there to clean and include the truly essential pieces for working toward your objectives.

◆ How often should you update your Vision Map? I suggest revisiting the Vision Map weekly. Ideally Monday and/or Friday you will return to the Vision Map to align on progress and changes to the map. We'll talk more about how to utilize the map in the Structure section.

◆ If you can motivate your team to embrace and participate in the creation and relevance of the Team Vision Map, your work together will become much easier and more enjoyable.

Awake Tip 1

Give Positive Acknowledgement

As a leader, especially as a new leader taking on an existing team, a big part of gaining the trust and respect of your team is giving acknowledgement. Positive acknowledgement cultivates a culture of connection and community. People don't need a constant stream of praise; however, when team members don't receive positive acknowledgement periodically for their contributions, they lose motivation and connection to the mission. Appreciation and encouragement serve as fuel. It's something easy and essential to do that is often overlooked by leaders.

Acknowledgement can be in the form of a "thank you for all your help" as you walk by their desk or finish a meeting. It can take the form of treating someone to coffee one afternoon. It can be in the form of recognition at a team meeting. When team members see that other team members' thoughts, ideas, and work are positively acknowledged (even just with a public "thank you for... this week."), others will follow.

Spread positive acknowledgement and don't play favorites. It shouldn't be too difficult since everyone has a role to play. Just look at your Vision Map for what to acknowledge people for! It's never too early to start acknowledging your team for the work they do. Try to give one thoughtful, positive acknowledgement per day.

A visionary leader is clear about what his or her responsibilities and objectives are, and takes ownership of the team's work scope to bring the Vision to reality.

2

Support

noun;

to promote the interests or cause of

to keep (something) going

material assistance.

Support

What is Support?

Support is the fuel for your Vision. A fountain cannot function without water in the reservoir. A team cannot work toward the Vision without the right Support. An Awake leader must develop awareness and understanding of the kind of people, environment, schedule, and practices that are optimal for working toward the Vision.

How does a leader gain and give Support?

The first step in gaining Support is knowing what truly fuels your best work. An Awake leader must understand his or own true needs and set the conditions for success.

Finding the Support that truly fuels your best work is challenging. It takes experience, observation, and reflection to really hone in on what supports your best work at any point in time. The wrong kind of people, environmental factors, or schedule parameters create unnecessary complexity and actually get in the way of working efficiently and enthusiastically.

You may need to break down barriers of fear and bureaucracy to really hone in on what Support you need. It's worth it. It's the only way. You have to be clear and honest about what you need. If your leader or organization is not supportive, then maybe a different organization would better fuel your best work.

By honing in on what truly supports your work and taking action to set the conditions for success, you lead by example in encouraging your team to do the same.

in Words

Why is Support a leadership vital?

Even with a crystal clear Vision, the team can't execute work toward the Vision without the right Support. Each person has to individually understand his or her own Support needs. The leader must understand his or her own Support needs and also ensure the team's Support needs are met.

By working through the Support exercises, you'll answer the questions: *What environment serves my best work? Who supports my best work? What work schedule supports my best work? What forms of communication with my leader and team members support my best work?* Let's begin answering these questions and set the conditions for successful work toward the Vision.

Support Exercises

The purpose of the Support exercises is to identify the Support you need to really fuel your work and fuel your team. We often assume that we're subject to fixed constraints and conditions in our workplaces and our lives. However, we sometimes must challenge the norms in favor of a more conducive level of Support. When we first bring awareness to the elements of our environment and interactions that aren't supporting our best work toward the Vision, we gain confidence to change them or to ask our leader for the Support we need. Never assume your leader will say No to a necessary change if it fuels better work toward the Vision and overall wellness for you and your team.

The purpose of the first exercise is to reflect on the Support you need in different areas of your work and life. In the second exercise, you'll begin taking those insights to action. In the final exercise, you'll learn how to do the same exercises with your team members so that you can help them cultivate the conditions for their best work toward the Vision.

Exercise 1: Support Reflection Prompts

Exercise 2: Support Analysis and Actions

Exercise 3: Supporting Your Team

Supplies

✎ Pencil or pen

Support

Exercise 1: Reflection Prompts

Answer the following prompts about your environment, personal space, communication, people, and schedule.

Your Workspace and Environment

As a leader, you have had work environments where you produced and contributed great work. When you think about the places where you have worked most productively, what place(s) come to mind? *A specific office, your home, a coffee shop…*

_____

_____

_____

_____

What qualities of this place(s) made it so conducive to working? How did you feel there?

_____

_____

_____

_____

Your Workspace and Environment

Do you have a favorite personal set up for your workspace? What objects are in your ideal personal workspace? *A specific type of computer, keyboard, coffee mug, photos, lava lamp...*

_____

_____

_____

_____

_____

Are there any distractions or uncomfortable aspects of your current workspace? What are they?

_____

_____

_____

_____

_____

Support

People

When you think of a supportive person in your past or present work life, who comes to mind? *A specific manager, peer, direct report...*

_____

_____

_____

When you think of a person that does not support your best work or make you feel your best, who comes to mind? Why?

_____

_____

_____

What qualities about the leadership style, mentoring style, tone of voice, or confidence of the person you admire stand out? How are they different from the person that does not support you and make you feel your best?

_____

_____

_____

_____

Communication

What are your primary methods of communicating with your leader and your peers at work?

_____

_____

_____

Do you feel the current method and frequency of communication with your leader are effective? Why or why not?

_____

_____

_____

_____

Who is someone that gives the right frequency and tone of communication? Who is someone that communicates too much or too little, or with a negative tone? What are the impacts of each approach?

_____

_____

_____

_____

Schedule

Are there certain rituals in your typical work day that you look forward to? What are your most important rituals? *Morning coffee, taking a walk, exercising, walking the dog, TV, reading…*

_____

_____

_____

_____

_____

Is there anything about your schedule that you would change if you could? If you could change one or more things about your daily or weekly schedule, what would you change?

_____

_____

_____

_____

_____

Exercise 2: Analysis and Actions

Look back at your answers from Exercise 1 as you work through the analysis prompts below.

We'll use a rating system to identify where to focus and how to prioritize. How would you rate your level of Support in the four areas **currently**? Use the scale below to circle the number you feel represents your level of Support in each area. 10 is the best ranking, 1 is the poorest ranking.

Workspace and Environment

1   2   3   4   5   6   7   8   9   10

People

1   2   3   4   5   6   7   8   9   10

Communication

1   2   3   4   5   6   7   8   9   10

Schedule

1   2   3   4   5   6   7   8   9   10

Support

Response

Refer to your ratings and answers to the Exercise 1 prompts. What is the area with the lowest rating that you need to focus on most to improve your level of Support?

_____

_____

_____

How will you begin to cultivate or ask for the Support you need to improve your conditions for working toward the Vision? Actions can include specific ways to change up your work environment. You could talk to your leader about changes you need to make or set new schedule parameters. Remember, do not settle for sub-optimal Support. Never assume change is not possible!

_____

_____

_____

_____

_____

Exercise 3: Supporting Your Team

Take your team through Exercise 1 and then have them do Exercise 2 on their own.

In each of your next one-on-one meetings with your team members, discuss their Exercise 2 answers if they want to share them and discuss with you. Share your answers with them, as well as the Support parameters you set up. Discuss what they can do themselves now and what you can give Support for. Maybe not all requests can be accommodated (you probably can't buy them a company car next week) but try to accommodate at least one environment modification or one schedule change. If something they point out cannot be accommodated, make sure you specify why it can't be accommodated and/or why you can't ask approval for it. If compensation concerns come up, handle it based on what you know is possible and appropriate. However, also note that improved team productivity could lead to higher compensation!

After talking with each member individually, discuss answers and actionable items at your next team meeting. Plan to hold each other accountable for adding these supportive elements you identified. The accountability is not just to keep each other on track but to support each other in creating a more conducive work environment to work toward the Vision!

This exercise opens dialog and a comfortable open communication between you and your team members, both one-on-one with you and as a team, about how to start moving toward a better support system for them. By prioritizing Support, you build relationships of trust with your team members and fuel the Vision.

Fill the reservoir.

Awake Tip 2

Give Feedback as Fuel

Giving and receiving feedback frequently and graciously is a huge part of Support. Feedback includes positive acknowledgement but it also includes the necessary compliment, which is constructive feedback. If the team is communicating in general, that is good and it probably means they are giving and receiving feedback from each other. If not, it's up to you to cultivate conversation and provide opportunities for giving and receiving constructive feedback during one-on-one meetings and team meetings.

Constructive feedback is important so that team members improve and the team can move forward with more strength. However, constructive feedback can bring up feelings of fear, non-acceptance, and judgment. To avoid discouraging your team members, always start with acknowledging something they did well and then segway into the constructive suggestions for future change or improvement. When they take action based on constructive feedback, more positive acknowledgement follows!

Some team members will constantly want feedback and others will be able to take just one piece of feedback each week to focus on. People have very different ways of communicating, as well as receiving and integrating feedback. As the leader, it's up to you to observe. If they are not integrating feedback into their work, talk about it with them at one-on-one meetings. Ask about what obstacles they may be encountering and encourage them to embrace feedback and try a new approach. Always enter conversations about constructive feedback with the intention of giving Support and facilitating collective progress.

A fountain cannot function without water in the reservoir.

A team cannot work toward the Vision without the right Support.

3

Structure

noun;

organization of parts as dominated by the
general character of the whole

the aggregate of elements of an entity in their
relationships to each other

Structure

What is Structure?

Once the Vision is clear and Support is in place, it's time to create the Structure for your Team Vision. Structure is the catalyst that takes your Vision from what to **how**.

Structure specifies who is doing what tasks and when tasks and projects must be completed in order for the team to accomplish objectives toward the Vision. Structure specifically refers to providing clear delegation and timelines for your team based on the Vision.

In Awake Leadership, Structure does not mean making and enforcing rules like what time to come into the office and what to wear. Most people have one of two opinions about this kind of classic Structure. Some people love lots of Structure at work. They love explicit rules. The second kind of person believes that rules are limiting, necessary evils that organizations set up to feel in control and limit Freedom. For most of my time as a leader and team member, I was in the second group. Most forms of Structure bothered me a lot! Why? Rules often created unnecessary complexity and limited potential. There was too much Structure in the form of rules that didn't really serve the work. However, I realized that Structure in the form of direction (delegation and timing specifications) and basic team rules do provide good guidelines for behavior and collaboration.

In this section, we'll focus on Structure as delegation and timing, and prioritize our actions toward the Vision. It's up to you to create basic team rules that serve and constantly reevaluate to make sure rules are enabling progress toward the Vision rather than limiting progress and autonomy.

Where does Structure come from?

The team Structure is set by the leader. Delegation and timing direction must be handed down from the leader to the team members in order to stay aligned as you work toward the Vision. By understanding your team's strengths and interests, you can delegate optimally. By understanding timing requests from your leader, you can plan timelines.

Why is Structure a leadership vital?

Structure is essential because it is how you keep your team aligned in action toward the Vision. Structure is how you articulate who is doing what tasks and when tasks and projects must be completed. Without Structure, the team doesn't know who should do what tasks and when tasks need to be completed. Structure allows the team to work more efficiently and removes confusion, redundant work, and frustration.

Vision and Structure enable alignment and create a platform for action. In the Structure exercises, you'll answer the questions: *Who should be doing what? When should that be done? How should I prioritize my tasks?* Let's begin the exercises.

Structure

in Action

Structure Exercises

Now that you have the Vision and Support in place, you can define the
Structure for how the tasks will be executed. You'll work through three
exercises to organize the delegation and timing of the tasks for your Vision.

The purpose of the first exercise is to prepare for delegation of the Vision
Map tasks and activities by gauging the skills, experience, strengths, and
interests of your team members. With deeper knowledge about these
qualities of your team members, you will be prepared to add delegation
and timing to the Vision Map in the second exercise. Finally, in the third
exercise, you'll learn a method for prioritizing the tasks on the Vision Map.

When you plan the work and articulate how you will collectively work
toward the Vision, the work becomes easier and more enjoyable. Let's
begin!

Exercise 1: Reflection

Exercise 2: Delegation and Timing

Exercise 3: Prioritization

Supplies

✎ Pencil or pen
✎ Your Vision Plan

Structure

Exercise 1: Reflection

This reflection will help you prepare for delegation of the team tasks and activities. Especially if you are onboarding new team members, this exercise will be useful for getting to know your team and delegating optimally. When team members are given tasks that match their skills, experience, strengths, and interests, they work more efficiently and enthusiastically toward the Vision.

Skills

Experience

Strengths

Interests

Begin with the prompts on the following page. Complete the reflection based on your knowledge about your team but also use the prompts as discussion questions for one-on-one meetings with team members to learn more about them. You should be well-versed in all four of these aspects of each team member as well as yourself!

Skills

Skills are your particular abilities related to your role. Skills relate to specific abilities or knowledge you have that allow you to execute actions for your work. What are Skills you have? What are your team's Skills?

_____

_____

_____

_____

_____

_____

_____

_____

_____

_____

Structure

Experience

Experience is where you have been - the positions, projects, and opportunities you have had related to your position that help inform and enhance your current work. What is your relevant experience? What is the relevant experience of each of your team members?

_____

_____

_____

_____

_____

_____

_____

_____

_____

_____

Strengths

Strengths are the qualities that make you an effective worker, contributor, and leader. While Skills are more tangible abilities, Strengths are descriptive qualities about you and your work style. What are your primary Strengths? What are the primary Strengths of each of your team members?

_____

_____

_____

_____

_____

_____

_____

_____

_____

_____

_____

Structure

Identifying Strengths: Strengths Finder Activity

Since identifying Strengths can be very subjective, I love this very organized assessment called StrengthsFinder 2.0. I recommend doing this with your team. Gallup StrengthsFinder 2.0 is an activity that can help you gauge how to delegate according to each person's strengths. This book and exercise is a great addition to your Strengths reflection and discussion because the test is a very thorough, well-put-together baseline assessment for learning about each person's strengths without a lot of guesswork and time. It is a very effective directional tool. It can also serve a fun team bonding activity for learning more about each other.

The Exercise

To do this exercise, first purchase the StrengthsFinder 2.0 books on Amazon or from the Gallup website. Each person on your team, including you, needs a book because you need a unique access code (in the back of the book) to each take the assessment online.

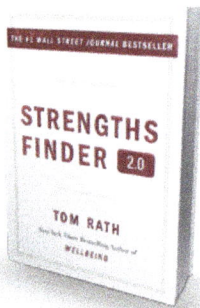

Take the assessment independently and have your team members each send their results - their five strengths - back to you. Make sure they do not reply all and send the results back to the whole team. If they do, it's okay, but it's more fun and insightful if you unveil the results during the team meeting. Once each person has taken the assessment and you have collected the results, unveil them at your team meeting. Discuss how many unique strengths your team has as a unit and discuss who has strengths in common. Revisit the strengths prompts and add your new insights based on the results.

Interests

Finally, Interests! Interests are maybe the most important piece of this reflection. Interests are what you want to learn or know more about. What about your work or organization makes you curious? What are the Interests of your team members?

_____

_____

_____

_____

_____

_____

_____

_____

_____

Structure

Exercise 2: Delegation and Timing

The Vision Map shows what your team does in action. The Vision Map with Structure details **how** your team will accomplish the Vision. Structure adds the essential detail including who does what and when things will happen. It's the full picture.

In this exercise, we'll add these two important components to your Vision Map: Timing and Delegation.

Why make a Team Vision Map with Structure?

The team can take focused, efficient action toward the Vision when they know who is responsible for what tasks and when they need to be accomplished.

As a leader, it is up to you to delegate tasks and observe if the task is really right for that person. You can use your Exercise 1 responses to determine the delegation of tasks. It takes tact, experimentation, and iteration to find the right delegation. Alignment of person with task based on strengths and interests can make work toward the Vision much more effective and efficient.

While delegation is up to your study and discernment, if you're a leader within an organization, timing is most often determined by your leader or the top-level leadership. This is because your team's contributions are based on the larger collective Vision of the organization. Timelines of projects should be discussed with your leader and then you can determine timing of sub-tasks from there.

Turn to the next page to begin adding delegation and timing to your Team Vision Map.

Adding Timing and Delegation to the Vision Map

Begin with your Team Vision Map from Section 1.

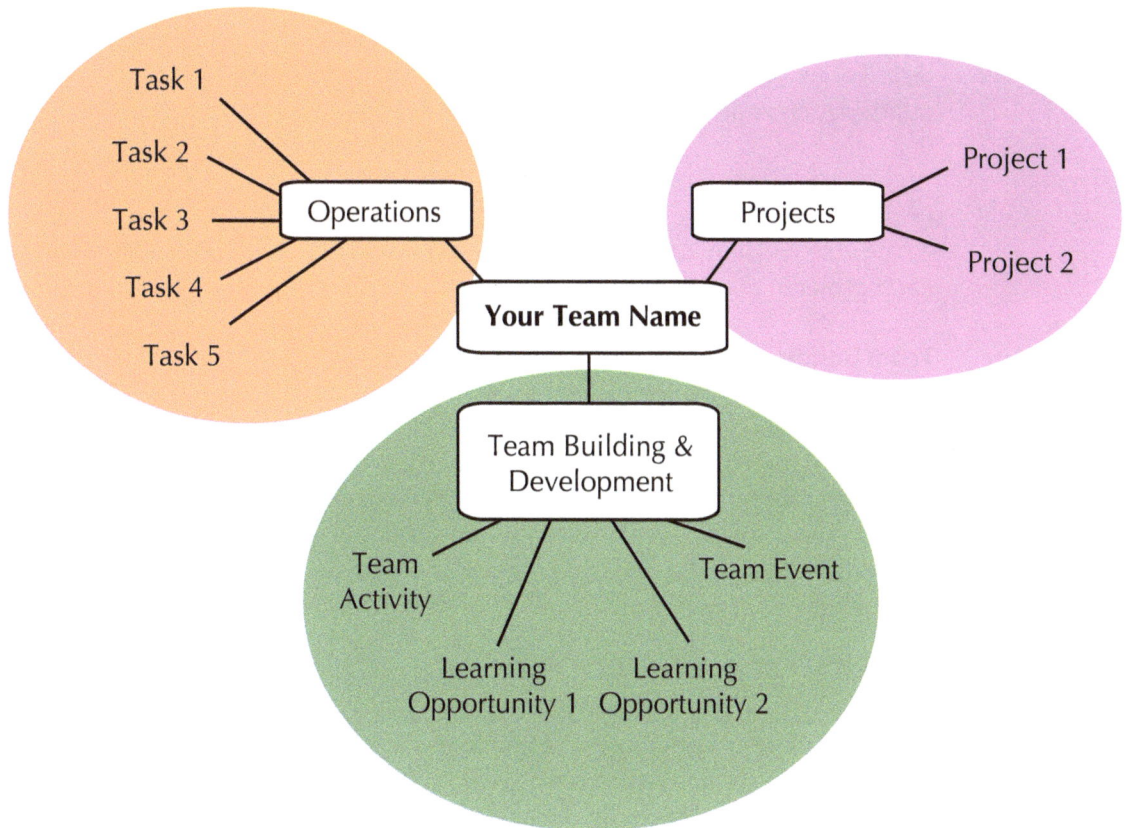

Task 1
Task 2
Task 3
Task 4
Task 5

Operations

Your Team Name

Projects

Project 1

Project 2

Team Building & Development

Team Activity

Learning Opportunity 1

Learning Opportunity 2

Team Event

Structure

Adding Timing and Delegation to the Vision Plan

Refer to the general Team Vision Map example on the following page to build layers 3 and 4.

Operations: First, add a branch to each task and assign the time basis of the task. For example, the time basis may be weekly, monthly, daily, or quarterly. Next, add a branch to assign the team member responsible for the task.

Projects: For Projects, the timing layer consists of the completion date for each project. Then add a branch to assign the team member responsible for each project.

Team Building and Development: To make the third layer, add the dates for the events and trainings. It's always best to get things on the calendar as early as possible so people can plan. For the fourth layer, assign yourself or a team member to each activity. This gives team members something different to focus on in terms of making sure people are aware of the event, own preparation, and make sure people show up. Try to give each team member at least one event or training to be involved in or accountable for participation and support. This also builds team culture and relationships.

Note on Delegation: It is important that every task, project, and team event is delegated to just one person. Distributing ultimate ownership among multiple people causes confusion and can jeopardize timely completion. I suggest having just one name associated with each for ultimate ownership, even if more than one person contributes.

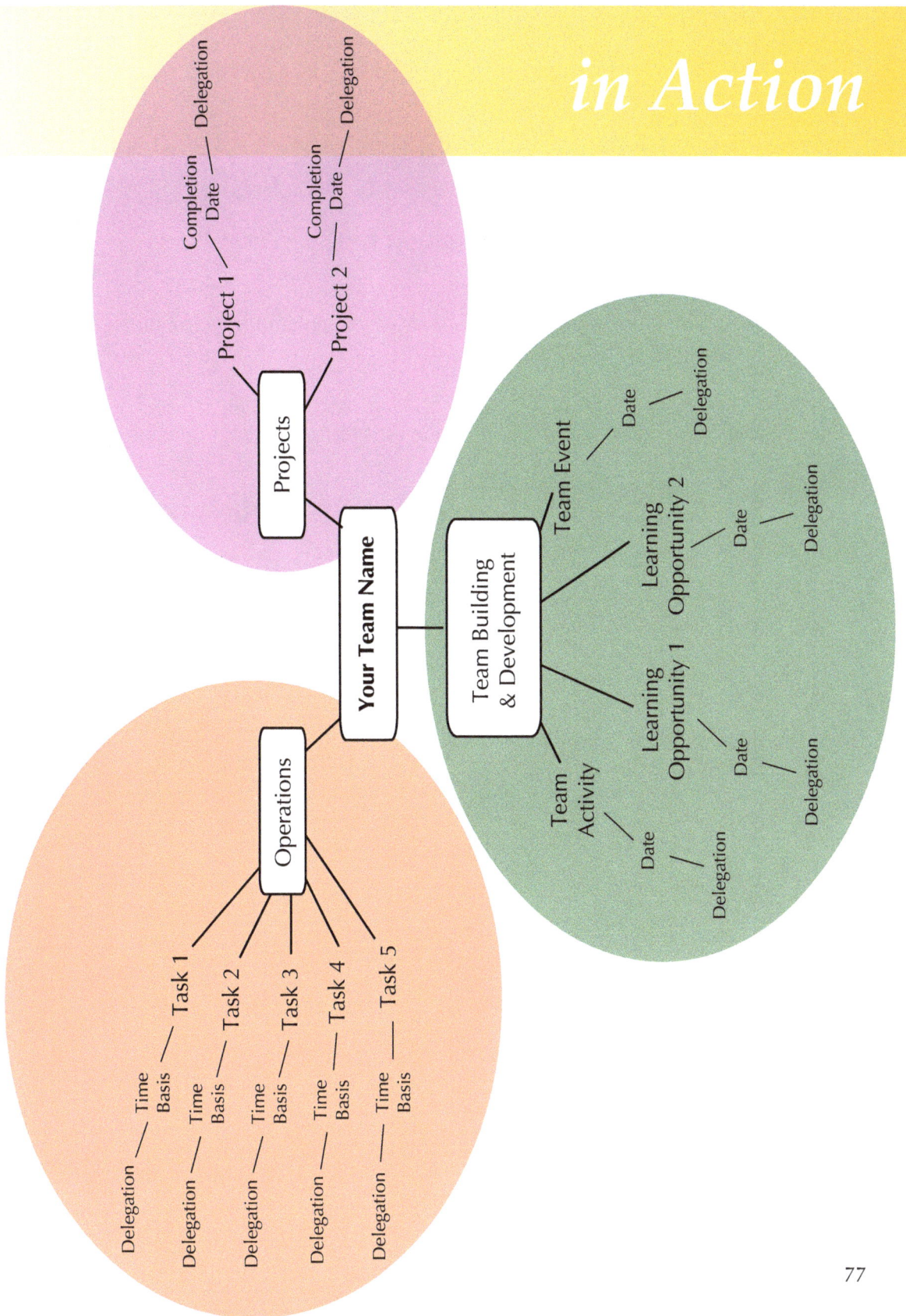

Your Team Name

Projects
- Project 1 — Completion Date — Delegation
- Project 2 — Completion Date — Delegation

Team Building & Development
- Team Event — Date — Delegation
- Learning Opportunity 2 — Date — Delegation
- Learning Opportunity 1 — Date — Delegation
- Team Activity — Date — Delegation

Operations
- Task 1 — Time Basis / Delegation
- Task 2 — Time Basis / Delegation
- Task 3 — Time Basis / Delegation
- Task 4 — Time Basis / Delegation
- Task 5 — Time Basis / Delegation

Structure

Adding Timing and Delegation to the Vision Plan

Let's look at Melanie's Team Vision Map example for how to build Structure layers 3 and 4.

Operations: First, Melanie added the time basis for all her operations. Next, she added the delegation of each task.

Projects: Next, Melanie added the target completion date for each project. She also added an owner for each project.

Team Building & Development: Finally, she added the event dates and a team member responsible for supporting each Team Building & Development activity or event.

Note: Adding delegation can at first be eye-opening. You can learn a lot about how tasks are distributed among the team. In this first pass, do it exactly as it truly is, now, and you can go back and redistribute after reviewing your draft.

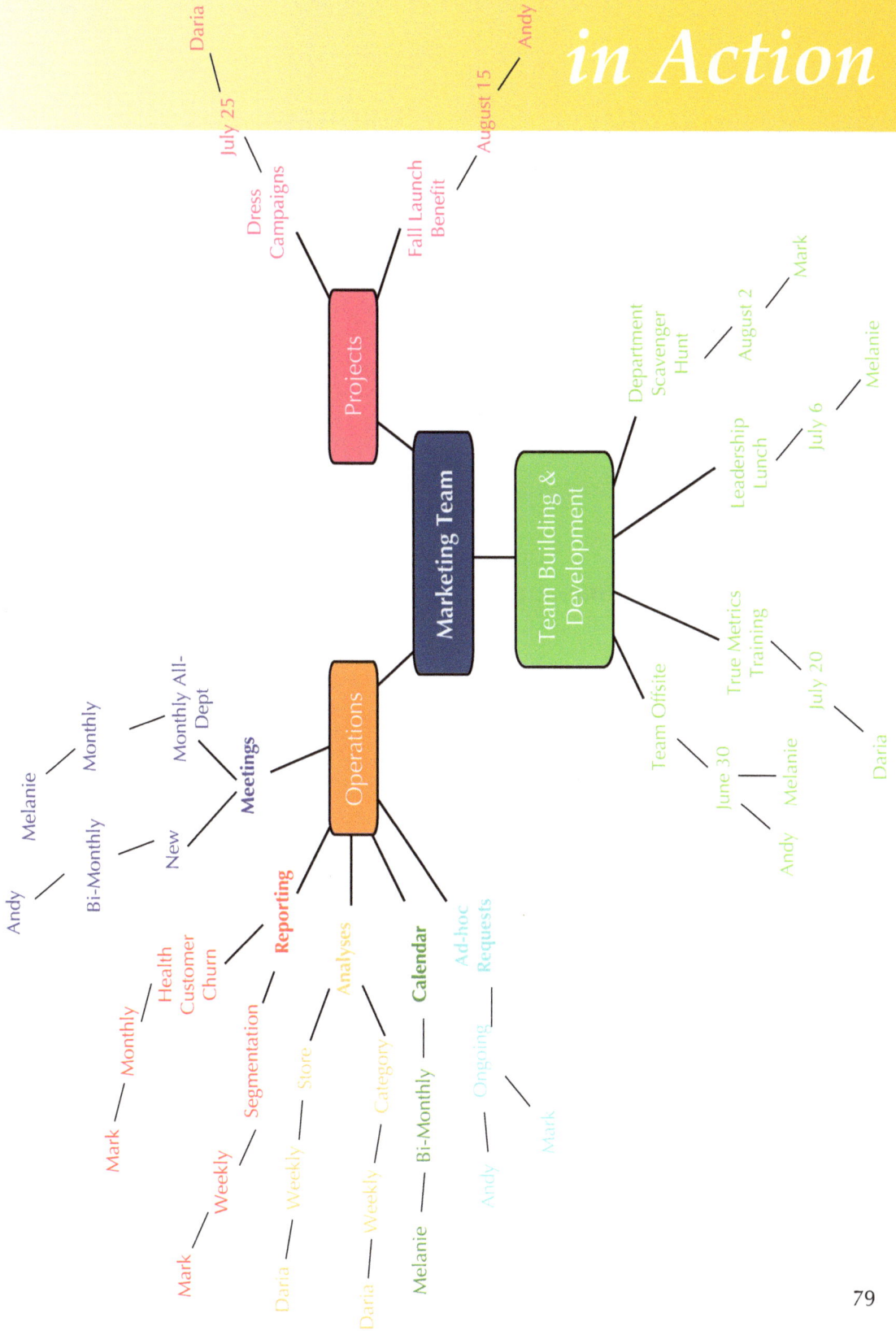

Projects
- Dress Campaigns — July 25 — Daria
- Fall Launch Benefit — August 15 — Andy

Marketing Team

Team Building & Development
- Department Scavenger Hunt — August 2 — Mark
- Leadership Lunch — July 6 — Melanie
- True Metrics Training — July 20 — Melanie — Daria
- Team Offsite — June 30 — Andy — Melanie

Operations
- Meetings
  - Monthly All-Dept
  - New — Bi-Monthly — Andy — Melanie — Monthly
- Reporting
  - Health Customer Churn — Monthly — Mark
  - Segmentation — Weekly — Mark
- Analyses
  - Store — Weekly — Daria
  - Category — Weekly — Daria
- Calendar
  - Bi-Monthly — Melanie
- Ad-hoc Requests
  - Ongoing — Andy
  - Mark

Structure

Your Turn!

Now it's your turn. You can do it! You already have the foundation.

Begin with your Team Vision Map and add layers 3 and 4 for timing and delegation. Use the example as guidance. There is additional Vision Map paper in the back of the book. If you need more space, use a white board, poster board, or digital Mind Mapping tool.

Tips for Making and Using Your Team Vision Map

◆ Make sure Operations have a consistent time basis and each Project has a completion date. This may make it clearer as to if you need to shift things from one branch to the other now if you were confused about what goes under Projects versus Operations.

◆ Review the final map with your team so that the time basis for Operations are correct and the completion dates for Projects are realistic. Also make sure the current delegation is accurate!

◆ The completed map will serve as a visual representation for how your team currently functions. All the essentials are there, clearly shown. Use the map as a discussion point with your leader and/or team members for determiing if work needs to be redistributed or clarified.

Exercise 3: The Action Plan

The Action Plan is a clear, step-by-step plan for how each person will take action this week. Leaders and team members often get stuck or procrastinate because the way forward isn't quite clear. When you have a clear plan of action, the work becomes more effortless. Let's prioritize in order to make your plan of action clear now based on the Vision Map.

There are three steps for taking the map into action.

Steps for Taking the Vision to Action

- ✔ Collect your Tasks and Activities

- ✔ Make your Action Plan

- ✔ Put Aside the Time

We'll make our Action Plan at the weekly level.

Turn to the next page to begin!

Structure

Collect Your Tasks and Activities

First, have each team member collect his or her tasks, projects, and activities from the Vision Map and list them out (you too!). Write the tasks down in a list on a piece of paper, in a notebook, or in a digital document.

Here is an example of what Daria's task list looks like. She has compiled all of her responsibilities from the Vision Map.

Daria's Tasks for this week:

☐ Store Analysis
☐ Category Analysis
☐ Remind team about training
☐ Work on next steps of Dress Campaign project

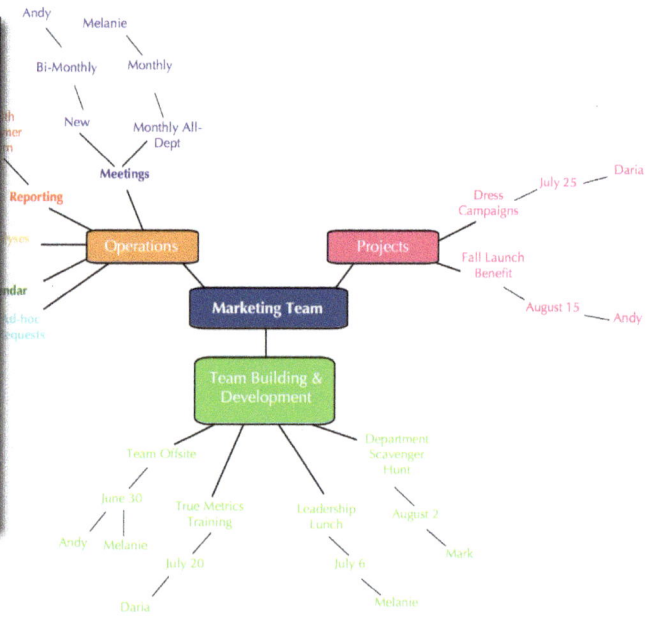

Make Your Action Plan

Next, according the task basis or project completion date, label the tasks that are most essential to complete this week with three stars, important tasks with two, and nice-to-have with just one.

You may need to make time to break down projects in more detail in order to do this. Help your team members with this in one-on-one touch bases. If you don't know, first practice discernment, of course. Think about what your leader would advise. Finally, if you need help in determining relative importance, ask your leader.

Below is Daria's example of her list with stars added.

Daria's Tasks for this week:

❏ Store Analysis ***
❏ Category Analysis ***
❏ Remind team about training **
❏ Work on next steps of Dress Campaign project *

Structure

Make Your Action Plan

Take your star list and next label the tasks by the day(s) of week that you will work on each. Work on the most important (3-star) tasks first and give them the most time in order to make sure they are completed.

Below is Daria's example of her list with days of the week added.

Daria's Tasks for this week:

❏ Store Analysis ***
❏ Category Analysis ***
❏ Remind team about training **
❏ Work on next steps of Dress Campaign project *

Daria's Tasks for this week:

❏ Store Analysis (Mon - Tues)
❏ Category Analysis (Wed - Thu)
❏ Remind team about training (Friday)
❏ Work on next steps of Dress Campaign project (Th - Friday)

Make Your Action Plan

On a new piece of paper or document, make your weekly schedule, starting with Monday. Under each day, place the tasks that you'll work on that day.

Now that Daria has her prioritized list, she can simply collect this week's tasks and put them into her Action Plan for the week.

Daria's Action Plan for this week:

Monday
- ☐ Store Analysis

Tuesday
- ☐ Complete Store Analysis

Wednesday
- ☐ Category Analysis

Thursday
- ☐ Complete Category Analysis
- ☐ Work on next steps of Dress Campaign project

Friday
- ☐ Remind team about training
- ☐ Work on next steps of Dress Campaign project

She reorganized and laid out the tasks by day of week to make her Action Plan for this week. It is a clear view of the week. She has translated her Vision Map tasks into an Action Plan.

Structure

Put Aside the Time

Now that you have planned the work, it's time to work the plan!

Are you ready? Let's take your Vision Map to action. Take your tasks for this week and make your Action Plan. Starting with your Team Vision Map, use Daria's example process as guidance. With a clear plan and the time, progress toward the Vision will happen.

Tips for Making and Using your Action Plan

◆ Is your workload realistic? Do you need to talk with your leader about how to prioritize? All tasks should **not** have three stars.

◆ Do you need to re-delegate the work? Re-delegate tasks if you need to redistribute the work. Try different approaches to delegation for weekly plans that balance realistic goals for progress with healthy challenge for your team.

◆ Did you find any redundant tasks or things that can be simplified? Keep this in mind as you make your Action Plan for yourself and with your team. You can do it!

Awake Tip 3

Respecting Time is Respecting People

I cannot emphasize enough my belief in the importance of being on time as a leader for meetings, regardless of whom the meeting is with or how important you feel it is. Being on time or communicating before the meeting if you cannot be there on time is paramount in respecting the people you work with. It's part of leading by example and working smarter, not harder. Use your time optimally and respect it. Respect for your own time and respect for the time of others is respect for the collective Vision. This is why it is important to intentionally place and accept each meeting on your calendar.

Before scheduling a meeting, send a meeting invite with a statement like, "The purpose of this meeting is..." and state a clear purpose. This will tether you and the group to the intention and objectives of the meeting. Don't send a meeting request without a description of purpose and an agenda. Especially for busy leaders, a purpose statement helps to remember what you'll do at the meeting and what to prepare. Time you waste for them is time wasted on accomplishing the collective Vision of the organization. Schedule meetings intentionally and show up a minute early. Show up prepared. Work toward mindfulness and proactive, transparent communication.

If you are leading a meeting and it ends early, don't apologize. Schedule meetings for as long or a little longer than you think the meeting will take. If you finish early, you have just given people back valuable time to go use on other tasks or to take a breath.

Structure specifies **who** is doing what tasks and **when** tasks and projects must be completed in order for the team to the accomplish objectives toward the Vision.

4

Tools

noun, plural;

devices that aid in accomplishing
a task(s)

instruments used in performing an operation or
necessary in the practice of a vocation or
profession

means to an end

Tools

What are Tools?

Tools are resources used to work toward the Vision. Tools serve as a means for doing your work and getting your work done. Tools serve as means for collaboration.

For organizations that make products, tools are used to make products and to procure and distribute goods. In the service industry, tools allow service providers to travel, enhance services, and enable communication.

How do you identify the right Tools?

As an Awake leader, it's important to identify tools that are most optimal for accomplishing your Vision tasks. Execution of tasks becomes more efficient with the right Tools and knowledge about how to use them.

There are two main challenges with Tools. The first challenge is determining which Tools to select and use. As technology advances and expands, more and more Tools are developed everyday. It's information and choice overload for leaders. You could constantly research and update your tool belt. The second challenge is making sure you and your team members have the right knowledge of how to use the Tools that you select. Sometimes the issue is not the Tool itself but how you use it.

As the leader, you select the Tools you need. With the right Tools and knowledge about how to use them, the work toward the Vision becomes more efficient and enjoyable.

Why are Tools a leadership vital?

Tools enable leaders to execute the Vision tasks. We can't execute the Vision tasks with our mind alone (at least I can't and I haven't seen it happen yet!). Tools are like extensions of our strengths and skills as a team. We need Tools to build, communicate, travel, and distribute products and services. Tools make tasks more efficient and enhance the quality of the work.

In the Tools exercises, you'll answer the questions: *Do we have the right Tools? Do we have too many Tools? Do we really know how to use the Tools we have?* If you feel you ask these questions often, the exercises in this section will help you to reevaluate and optimize your tool belt. You'll learn a method for periodically evaluating your tool belt as a team to work with more efficiency, ease, and enthusiasm! Let's get started.

Tools Exercises

The Tools exercises progression is a series of four exercises that should be worked in order. The purpose of this exercise progression is to look closely at your current Tools in order to uncover opportunities to optimize your tool belt. The Tools you use should not only simplify your work processes and make them more efficient, but they should also be enjoyable to use. Joy makes the work sustainable and enhances the quality of your results.

This is one of the most involved, challenging exercise sections but also very worth it. These exercises will show you how to filter, align, and strengthen your tool belt to better accomplish your Vision!

Exercise 1: Map Your Tool Belt

Exercise 2: Tools Matrix Set Up

Exercise 3: Complete the Matrix

Exercise 4: Analysis and Optimization

Supplies

- Pencil or pen
- Paper or computer-based spreadsheet
- Your Team Vision Map

Tools

Exercise 1: Map Your Tool Belt

In this first exercise, you'll take an inventory of all the Tools you use and what you use them for. Take out your Vision Map from Section 1 (the Vision Map without the Structure added, just the tasks).

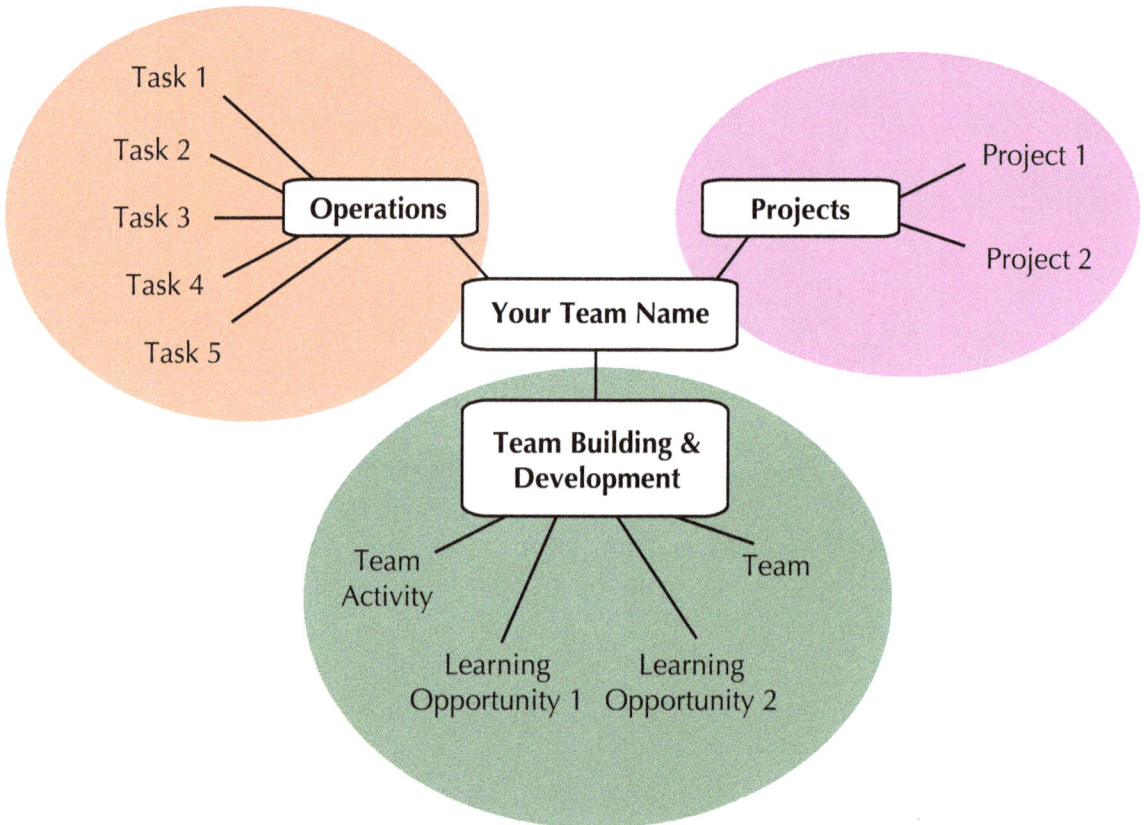

Task 1
Task 2
Task 3 — **Operations**
Task 4
Task 5

Projects
Project 1
Project 2

Your Team Name

Team Building & Development

Team Activity
Team

Learning Opportunity 1
Learning Opportunity 2

In the third layer, for each task, write down what Tool(s) you use to do each task. See the following page for a general example. It's okay if you repeat Tools. Some Tools are probably used for more than just one task.

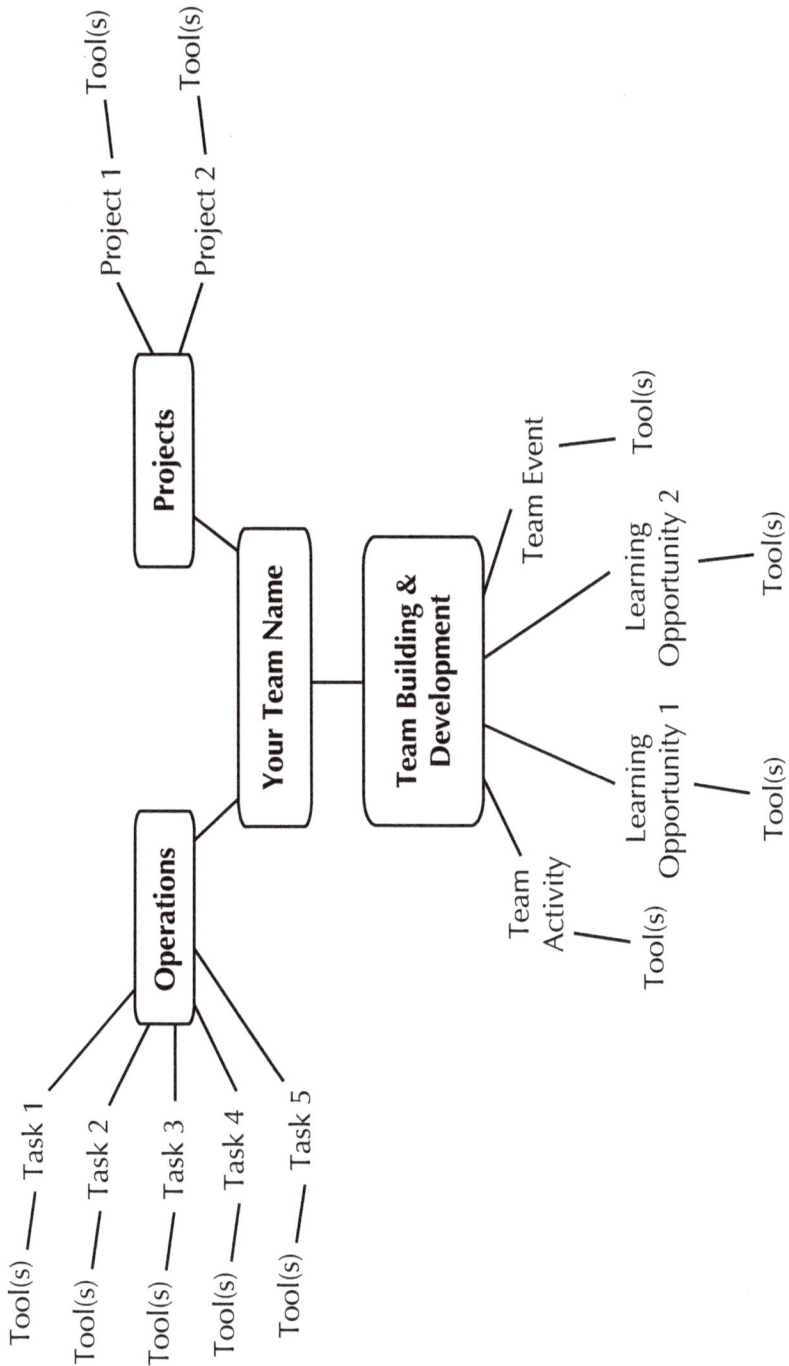

Tools

Marketing Team Example

Refer to Melanie's example on the following page. Melanie and her team members added all the Tools used for each task.

Operations: You can see that most of the Marketing Team's responsibilities that are operational are analytical. They primarily use analytical tools and presentation tools for their tasks.

Projects: For projects, they use similar analytical tools plus marketing planning and design tools.

Team Building and Development: There are not many Tools needed for team building and development since they are mainly attending events but they do need some!

As you can see on Melanie's map, many of the Tools are used for more than one task.

We'll get more into the analysis of the Tools they use in a later exercise. The purpose of this first exercise is just to make sure you have every Tool that you use for each task on the map.

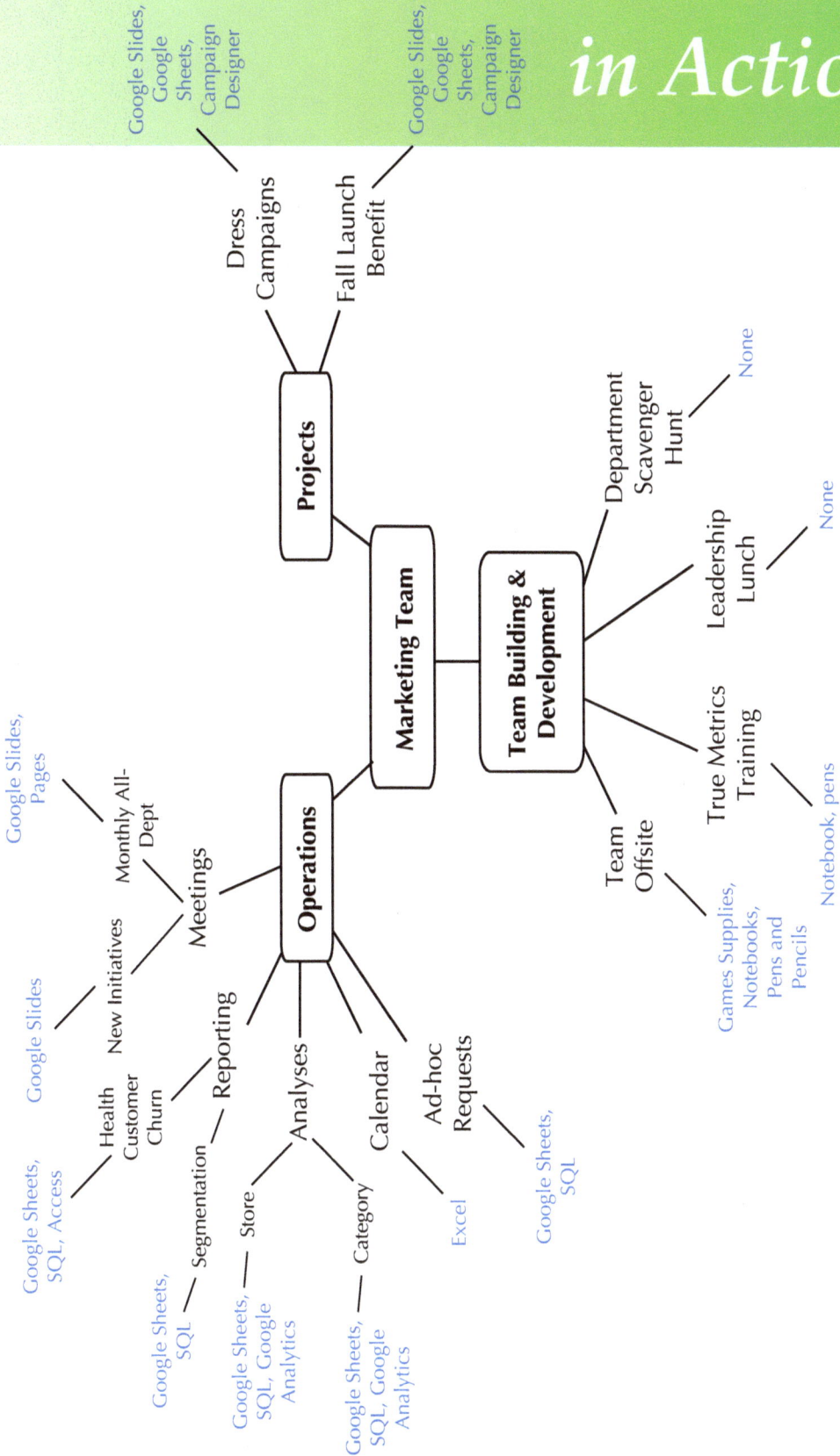

Marketing Team

Projects
- Campaigns
  - Dress — Google Slides, Google Sheets, Campaign Designer
- Fall Launch Benefit — Google Slides, Google Sheets, Campaign Designer

Team Building & Development
- Department Scavenger Hunt — None
- Leadership Lunch — None
- True Metrics Training — Notebook, pens
- Team Offsite — Games Supplies, Notebooks, Pens and Pencils

Operations
- Meetings
  - Monthly All-Dept — Google Slides, Pages
  - New Initiatives — Google Slides
- Reporting
  - Health Customer Churn — Google Sheets, SQL, Access
  - Segmentation — Google Sheets, SQL
- Analyses
  - Store — Google Sheets, SQL, Google Analytics
  - Category — Google Sheets, SQL, Google Analytics
- Calendar — Excel
- Ad-hoc Requests — Google Sheets, SQL

Tools

Your Turn!

Return to your Team Vision Map from Section 1 and begin branching to add the Tools used for each task. Refer to the Marketing Team's example for guidance. You can use the additional Team Vision Map paper in the back of the book, a digital spreadsheet, or slides.

Notes: You may feel as though you have many more Tools than the Marketing Team's example. That is okay and even more reason to do this exercise. As we move through the exercise, you'll see how working through this will uncover opportunities for simplifying and gaining clarity.

Exercise 2: Tools Matrix Set Up

In this second exercise in the progression, you will make your Tools Matrix. You'll set up your Tools Matrix using your map from Exercise 1.

To begin, open a a digital spreadsheet or make a hand-drawn table like the table below.

Tools Matrix					

Tools

Marketing Team Tools Matrix

Tasks	Tools							
	Access	Campaign Designer	Excel	Google Analytics	Google Sheets	Google Slides	SQL	Notebook/Pen
Monthly All-Dept Meeting								
New Initiatives Meeting								
Health Customer Churn Report								
Segmentation Report								
Store Analysis								
Category Analysis								
Calendar								
Ad-Hoc Requests								
Dress Campaigns Projects								
Fall Launch Benefit Project								
Team Offsite								
True Metrics Training								
Leadership Lunch								
Department Scavenger Hunt								

Tools Matrix Set Up

In the first column of the table, list all of your tasks.

In the first row of the table, list all of your unique Tools. Make sure each Tool is just listed once.

Refer to the example of the Marketing Team's Tools Matrix on the opposite page as you set up your matrix. As you can see from the example, Melanie and her Marketing Team have placed all their tasks along the first column and all their Tools along the first row to make their Tools Matrix.

This is all you need to do in order to complete Exercise 2.

Your Turn!

Using your Vision Map and an empty table or spreadsheet, set up your team's Tools Matrix. Make sure each Tool and each task is just listed once.

Tools

Exercise 3: Complete the Matrix

The purpose of the matrix and ranking is to identify opportunities to simplify or add to your tool belt. To make the Tools Matrix functional and prepare for analysis, in this exercise you'll add Rankings and Utilization Scores to the Tools Matrix.

Ranking

The ranking of a Tool signifies how efficient an easy the Tool is to use.

Put a number next to each relevant task-tool combination in your Tools Matrix, based on the corresponding ranking scheme:

> 1   The team feels they know how to use the Tools for the task and that it accomplishes the task efficiently
>
> 2   The team feels they know how to use the Tool for that task but it does not help to efficiently accomplish the task toward the Vision
>
> 3   The team feels they don't fully know how to use the Tool for the task

On the next page, you'll see the Marketing Team's Tools Matrix with rankings added.

Marketing Team Tools Matrix

Tasks	Access	Campaign Designer	Excel	Google Analytics	Google Sheets	Google Slides	Pages	SQL	Notebook/Pen
Monthly All-Dept Meeting						1	1		
New Initiatives Meeting	2					1			
Health Customer Churn Report					1			1	
Segmentation Report					1			1	
Store Analysis				3	1			1	
Category Analysis				3	1			1	
Calendar			1						
Ad-Hoc Requests					1			1	
Dress Campaigns Projects		1			1	1			
Fall Launch Benefit Project		1			1	1			
Team Offsite									1
True Metrics Training									1
Leadership Lunch									
Department Scavenger Hunt									

Tools

Utilization Score

To complete your Tools Matrix, you'll next compute the Utilization Score for each Tool. While the ranking signifies how efficient and easy to use a Tool is, the Utilization Score shows how prevalent or important it is for your team. The Utilization Score is a signifier or metric for how much use you get out of each of your Tools. Of course, some tasks may be important than others, but for this exercise, all tasks are considered equal importance and this is at least a starting point of conversation for the team to discuss Tools opportunities in the next exercise.

To compute the Utilization Score, count the number of tasks you use each Tool for. Place the total count at the bottom of each column for the Tool. Do not add up the rankings, just count the number of tasks the Tool is used for. This makes sense since the Utilization Score is showing how relevant the tool is for the team.

On the next page, you'll see the Marketing Team's Tools Matrix with Rankings and Utilization Scores added. Just to point out one specific example, notice how Google Analytics is used for two tasks, so the Utilization Score is 2.

Stick with the process and follow through! You're almost to the satisfying results part.

Marketing Team Tools Matrix

Tasks	Tools								
	Access	Campaign Designer	Excel	Google Analytics	Google Sheets	Google Slides	Pages	SQL	Notebook/Pen
Monthly All-Dept Meeting						1	1		
New Initiatives Meeting						1			
Health Customer Churn Report	2				1			1	
Segmentation Report					1			1	
Store Analysis				3	1			1	
Category Analysis				3	1			1	
Calendar			1						
Ad-Hoc Requests					1			1	
Dress Campaigns Projects		1			1	1			
Fall Launch Benefit Project		1			1	1			
Team Offsite									1
True Metrics Training									1
Leadership Lunch									
Department Scavenger Hunt									
Utilization Score -->	1	2	1	2	7	4	1	5	2

Tools

Your Turn!

Now it's your turn to add the Rankings and Utilization Scores for each Tool in order to complete your Tools Matrix. Start by placing the Ranking for each task-tool combination in your matrix.

Tips for Completing Your Tools Matrix

◆ Complete the matrix with your team. This is a great team activity to get everyone on the same page about the use of your Tools and any blind spots. The team member(s) that use the Tool associated with each task should give input as to what the Ranking should be.

◆ Though doing the Rankings and computing the Utilization score may seem formal and technical, remember that this process really represents a way of thinking about your Tools. Rankings and Utilization Score put a label to the process of thinking about your tool belt in terms of which Tools could be replaced or eliminated and which Tools are you most valuable. By going through this process, you gain awareness and insights about how to optimize your tool belt.

Great job making it this far in a challenging section! Now let's move on to the final Tools exercise to enjoy looking at the results and identify opportunities.

Exercise 4: Analysis and Optimization

The previous three exercises were for setting up the foundation for looking at your team's tool belt with collective clarity. We'll use your completed Tools Matrix to do analysis and optimization in this exercise. The purpose of this exercise is to bring it all together and identify opportunities to simplify your tool belt. You'll identify opportunities for making your tool belt more efficient in terms of time and cost. You'll identify where you may need to add or change Tools. You'll identify where team members need more training in order to better execute tasks with efficiency and enjoyment.

Training Opportunities

Training is so important for tasks to be done efficiently and accurately and for team members to feel set for success. In most cases, it is much more economical to send a current employee to train on a Tool than to hire a new person who needs to learn the other aspects of the role and the organization. On your Tools Matrix, first identify the task-tool cells you marked with a **3** ranking. List the Tools where your team identified they need training and list them in order of highest to lowest utilization score to prioritize which ones to look for training on first. Which tools did your team mark with a ranking of **3**? Who is responsible for the task associated?

_____

_____

_____

_____

Tools

Replacement or Addition Opportunities

Identify the task-tool cells with a 2 ranking. Sort the Tools in order of highest to lowest Utilization Score. Which tools did you rank with a 2? Who is responsible for the task associated?

_____

_____

_____

_____

Making the Plan

For Tools with a rank of 3, the strategy is to make a training plan for the person that uses that tool. First identify who (based on your Vision Map with Structure) is responsible for that task. There many ways to plan a training: You can partner that person with a team member that knows the Tool well, you can train them (if you know the tool well), or send them to a training.

For Tools with a ranking of 2, there are a few ways to consider optimizations and these should be discussed with your team members, especially the team members that use the Tools. The first strategy is to replace the Tool with another you have in your tool belt that can perform the task. The second strategy is to research outside for a better, additional Tool to acquire.

Example from the Marketing Team

Melanie sought input from her team members to rank the tool-task combinations and found two opportunities for improvements. The summary of her Exercises 4 opportunities for action is on the next page.

Training

First, Daria pointed out that she didn't feel fully trained on Google Analytics. Melanie and Daria decided that Melanie would train Daria on Google Analytics this month and that Daria would attend a training off-site to learn more and ask questions.

Replacement Opportunities

Secondly, Mark pointed out that Access (a data management tool) made it difficult and cumbersome for him to do his Health Customer Churn report. Melanie and Mark agreed that it would be better to take the time to transfer that data table into SQL (a more optimal data management tool) to simplify their tool belt and make the task more efficient.

From this analysis and planning, the Marketing team both found a training opportunity and an opportunity to simplify their tool belt for more efficiency and ease.

Tools

Example from the Marketing Team

Marketing Team Tools Optimization

Tools marked with Rank of 3: **Google Analytics**

Task: Store Analysis, Category Analysis

Person responsible for this task: **Daria**

Plan: Daria will <u>train</u> with Melanie on Google Analytics and attend a Google Analytics training off-site to learn the latest applications and ask more questions

Tools marked with Rank of 2: **Access**

Task: Health Customer Churn Report

Person responsible for this task: **Mark**

Plan: Instead of keeping one important data table in Access, we'll transfer the data table to SQL to optimize our tool belt and make our data systems more organized and easy to use. We'll <u>replace</u> Access with SQL for this task.

in Action

Your Turn!

Use the following prompts to make your Tools Optimization Plan.

Tools marked with Rank of **3**: _____

Task(s): _____

Person(s) responsible for this task: _____

Plan: _____

_____

Tools marked with Rank of **2**: _____

Task(s): _____

Person(s) responsible for this task: _____

Plan: _____

_____

Awake Tip 4

Follow Through

Taking action and closing the loop on commitments and plans is essential for leaders to do. Following through is important because when we follow through, we reach our objectives, we learn, and we lead by example for others to do the same. For teams, a culture of follow through cultivates trust and respect. There is no short cut or way around it; the only way is through.

Sometimes it feels impossible to follow through on a tough project or commitment. If you find that, along the way, an objective or plan actually has negative, unintended consequences, then abandoning it is likely the right choice. However, building the discipline and drive to follow through in the face of challenge is essential for growth and evolution. Leaders must walk the talk. Great ideas and plans must be implemented. By planning and committing from a place of clarity, your intentions are solid and it's easier to follow through. This is what we worked on in sections 1 through 4.

With your Team Vision Map structured and your Tools opportunities planned, make sure to take action and follow through. You have planned the work and now it's time to work the plan!

Tools are like extensions of our strengths and skills. The right tools help teams manifest the Vision optimally.

5

Context

noun;

the interrelated conditions in which something
exists or occurs

Context

What is Context?

Context is knowledge and understanding of the overall organization beyond your own team. Context is where we zoom out to understand the reach and impacts of your Vision. Context allows the team to understand where your team contributions fit into the bigger picture. When you explore and immerse in Context, you return to your day-to-day work with new perspective and clarity about your purpose.

Where does Context understanding come from?

We learn Context through experience in the field, meeting people outside of our immediate team, and immersion in the organization. To understand Context, team members cannot work in a vacuum. Cross-functional work and immersions are required to gain understanding of Context. Immersion involves expanding your perspective through cross-functional projects, cross-functional trainings, meeting with people outside of your team, or shadowing other teams. We learn Context by observing how different functions of the business intersect and contribute toward the overall Vision.

Why is Context a leadership vital?

The team will work toward the Vision more optimally if they have an understanding of the organization as a whole; how it works and the impacts. When you see how your work impacts the whole, you can better tailor it to the overall Vision objectives and needs of other teams. Knowledge about Context not only improves your work but also provides appreciation and peace of mind for team members because they can see how their contributions are implemented and appreciated by others in the organization. An organization is a living system, constantly changing, but each day you should strive to learn a little more about how it works and stay informed as it changes and evolves.

This section is about zooming out. An Awake leader can zoom in on their own Vision and zoom out to see how it relates to and impacts the big picture. It's all connected. The Context exercises will help you answer the questions: *How does my team fit into the bigger picture? How do my contributions and day-to-day work impact the organization? What other opportunities are there within the organization beyond my current realm? How can I meet other cool people in the organization that share the same interests but have different skills and experience?*

Let's begin the exercises to provide Context for your team members and yourself!

in Action

Context Exercises

The purpose of the Context exercises is to understand gaps in knowledge your team may have about their work and the organization. You'll zoom out to understand the landscape of the whole organization and where your team fits in. You'll immerse your team in other areas of the organization so they can better understand what other functions do and how their work relates to the whole.

Exercise 1: Field Notes

Exercise 2: Organization Landscape

Exercise 3: Immersion Trips

Supplies

- Pencil or pen
- Journals or notebooks (one for each team member, including yourself)
- Graph paper or computer-based spreadsheet
- Dry Erase Board and markers

Context

Exercise 1: Field Notes

Field Notes is a simple exercise for bringing awareness to gaps in knowledge and identifying where to begin exploring to get answers. This exercise will help you to gauge the team's blind spots so you can help them cultivate knowledge that helps them execute their tasks toward the Vision with more ease and efficiency. You will do this by prompting inquiry and by encouraging open communication and discussion.

The Exercise

It's helpful to buy your team dedicated field notes journals or notebooks to make the activity official and structured. Introduce the exercise in Monday meeting and ask that, as they go about their week, they each write down three questions to share with the team at Friday meeting. These questions can be about the organization, systems you use, or their work tasks. They can find the answer before Friday meeting from a subject matter expert in the company or on their own. Otherwise, ask that they bring the question on Friday unanswered and work together as a team to answer the question.

Note: To reiterate, it is helpful to purchase a dedicated notebook because it emphasizes the importance of the exercise and gives team members a place to put these thoughts specifically. Make it a priority. Do this exercise for three weeks in a row and, if it seems helpful, continue forever!

See the next page for an example of Field Notes.

Marketing Team Example

Field Notes Questions: Daria - Marketing Analyst

Why do we send out promotional e-mail on Mondays and Fridays?

Who makes updates to customer orders and special requests after the order has been placed?

Who uses the Segmentation Report? What happens with it after we send it to the leadership team?

Do our products undergo quality inspections? Where does that happen?

Context

Your Turn!

Purchase Field Notes journals and initiate the exercise with your team.

<u>Note</u>: You may be thinking: *But my team never has any questions! They are so quiet and will just shake their heads*. Don't give up! It starts with one. If you bring questions or prompt questions, the team will join in. It's about tapping into curiosity. Many people are afraid to ask questions because it may seem like they aren't qualified or knowledgeable. However, if you as the leader encourage curiosity and inquiry, the team will open up to it. If you lead by example and prompt each of them to start with one question about their work or another department, it's progress. A curious team is an engaged team. You can provide the Marketing Team example questions to get them started.

Exercise 2: Organization Landscape

As a lover of arts and crafts, this is one of my favorite activities. The purpose of this exercise is to gain understanding and perspective of the organization as a whole. When the team understands the full context of the organization and how their work fits in, a new appreciation and engagement (and maybe more Field Notes questions!) follow.

To do this, you will make a 2D or 3D model of the organization's physical landscape. This is a great activity to do as a team at a Friday meeting. This can also be used as a piece of functional artwork to display in the office. It's fun to do this exercise annually to see how the organization changes and evolves.

Check out the following pages for the step-by-step instructions and examples for making your landscape.

<u>Note</u>: I suggest doing this exercise as more of an arts and crafts project (as opposed to digitally) because it's meant for educational purposes but also as a team bonding activity. Stand up, get away from your desk, and get creative!

Context

Document the Facilities

The first step for creating your landscape is to make the plan. Open a new spreadsheet document or take out a blank sheet of paper. List all the physical facilities or locations in your organization's physical network.

If you work for an educational organization, this might consist of all the buildings or facilities on campus or in the network. If you work for a medical organization, this list might consist of all the hospitals and related facilities. If you work in retail, this might consist of all the stores, offices, and production facilities.

Example Locations List

Location	City and State
Home Office	San Diego, CA
Vendor 1	San Francisco, CA
Vendor 2	Reno, NV
Vendor 3	Albuquerque, NM
Vendor 4	Helena, AR
Vendor 5	Detroit, MN
Vendor 6	High Point, NC
Inventory Center 1	Philadelphia, PA
Inventory Center 2	Dallas, TX
Inventory Center 3	Los Angeles, CA
Store 1	Portland, OR
Store 2	Santa Barbara, CA
Store 3	Maui, HI
Store 4	New Orleans, LA
Store 5	New York, NY

Note: The color coding by location type is optional. I just color coded so you can follow my example and it's how I like to organize.

Collect Your Supplies

The second step is to collect your supplies. Below are some ideas for supplies you could use to make your landscape.

Sample Landscape Foundation:

◆ Whiteboard
◆ Poster Board
◆ Cork Board

Sample Facility Pieces:

◆ Magnets
◆ Stickers
◆ Thumb tacks

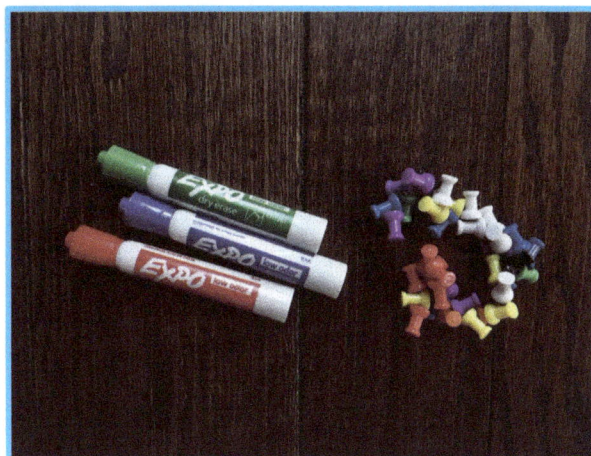

Get creative with your supplies!

Assemble

Using your locations list and supplies, work together as a team to assemble your landscape.

Example of a Finished Organization Landscape!

Discussion and Display

Finally, now that you have completed your landscape, find a place to display your landscape and discuss with your team:

◆ What did you learn about the company network structure that you didn't previously know?

◆ How many different locations nationally or worldwide do you work with and/or talk with each day?

◆ Are there any locations you are particularly curious about? Why?

◆ Do you have any new questions about the organization after doing this exercise?

Your Turn!

Following the steps and using the landscape example for guidance, make your own landscape with your team.

Context

Exercise 3: Immersion Trips

Immersion Trips are amazing for giving team members a real understanding and appreciation for different areas of the organization. Immersion Trips and experiences allow the team members to learn more about the organization and connect with people they don't work with everyday. Others in the organization often have insights to help with your work, too.

An ideal Immersion Trip is one that connects you with the customers, end-users, partners, or co-workers. As you venture out on your Immersion Trips, observe how customers use and appreciate the products or services you provide. Observe what others in the company do and the tools they use for their work. Write this down in your Field Notes and, as a team, discuss your learnings. Consider making a team slide show after the trip to recap what you learned.

Examples of Immersion Trips

◆ If you work in retail at the Home Office, work in a store for a day or take a production facility tour

◆ If you work in retail at the store, shadow someone at the Home Office for the day or tour a production facility

◆ If you are an administrator, work or shadow an operational position for a day.

◆ If you work in an operational role, shadow an administration team member for a day.

Your Turn!

Use the prompts below to brainstorm and plan Immersion Trips for your team. You can also look at your Field Notes and Landscape model for ideas.

What areas of the organization are you curious to learn more about?

_____

_____

_____

_____

What off-site facilities would be interesting and informative for your team to visit and learn more about?

_____

_____

_____

_____

Awake Tip 5

Believe in the Power of the People

As we discussed in the Context exercises, you can gain valuable new ideas from talking with and sharing ideas with people outside of your immediate team. Other people have different knowledge and perspective on the company and beyond. By meeting new people, you also build your personal network.

People join and leave organizations frequently, for all different reasons, but I still stay in touch with people from all stages throughout my career and it has proven valuable in so many ways. People have given me recommendations, helped with questions about my work, and many have become personal friends.

While on your Immersion Trips, go with the intention of building and strengthening relationships with people you meet. Show up, ask questions, keep an open mind, and learn as much as possible. You could learn something far beyond your initial intention for the trip or make a life-changing connection. You never know what is possible!

When you explore and immerse in Context, you return to your day-to-day work with new perspective and clarity about your purpose.

6

Inspiration

noun;

the action or power of moving the intellect or emotions

the act of drawing in; specifically: the drawing of air into the lungs

the quality or state of being that has an animating or exalting effect

Inspiration

What is Inspiration?

Inspiration is fuel for your best work toward the Vision. It is also essential for gaining fresh ideas that help you enhance and evolve your work and life. When we seek out the right Inspiration, it moves us beyond basic Support and provides motivation and new energy for the Vision. Inspiration comes in the form of guidance, ideas, new knowledge, and even art.

While Support is about things that stabilize and fuel your best work, Inspiration is about what propels you work and life forward toward new potential. Inspiration is expansive. This is an important vital for Awake Leaders because, in order to come up with solutions and new ideas, you must constantly learn and synthesize new information and experiences.

Where does inspiration come from?

For Awake leaders, sources of Inspiration are usually influencers, authors, mentors, or learning and development opportunities. Each person draws Inspiration from different sources. You may have a great mentor in your organization that is inspiring. When you explore outside your own realm of work or outside the organization, new and different ways to approach your work and your progression emerge. Awake leaders are inspirational because they have found sources of Inspiration themselves. This Inspiration fuels their work and their ability to inspire the team.

Why is Inspiration a leadership vital?

Inspiration is expansive. Inspiration is refreshing. Inspiration is motivational. Many times when we work in the same office doing the same work with the same people day-to-day, we get down in the weeds and things start to feel redundant or stagnant. Our approaches and processes become outdated. Our growth stagnates. Inspiration gives you and your team members new ideas and motivation for shaping and executing your Vision.

Great sources of Inspiration provides ideas for new growth opportunities and ways to collaborate. Inspiration helps us tap into our creativity and motivation, which helps creative leaders make progress and helps structured, technical leaders practice more expansive, creative thinking. Inspiration helps leaders practice open mindedness and synthesis of ideas, which aid in problem solving.

The Inspiration exercises will help you answer the questions: *Where can I find inspiration? How can I become an inspirational leader? What is inspiration versus distraction?* You'll learn how to find fresh sources of Inspiration. You'll learn how to inspire your team members. Let's get started!

Inspiration

Inspiration Exercises

In the Inspiration exercises, you'll identify your sources of Inspiration and make a plan for how to cultivate new Inspiration. You will gain new ideas for how to improve and take your leadership of your work, team, and life to the next level. Inspiration gives you ideas and motivation for how to progress along your authentic path and encourage your team members to do the same.

Through the three Inspiration exercises, you will develop ideas and a plan for how to cultivate Inspiration for yourself and for your team. You'll start with where you are by reflecting on your current sources of Inspiration. Then, in the second exercise, you'll expand your current realm of Inspiration. In the third exercise, you'll learn exercises for inspiring your team and giving them inspirational opportunities.

Exercise 1: Reflection on Your Sources of Inspiration

Exercise 2: Expand Your Sources of Inspiration

Exercise 3: Team Exercises for Inspiration

Supplies

✎ Pencil or pen
✎ Paper
✎ Notebook

Inspiration

Exercise 1: Reflection

In the Support exercises, you wrote about what environments, people, communication, and schedule parameters give you fuel to accomplish your best work. In this first Inspiration exercise, you'll reflect on what environments, people, things, and experiences inspire you.

Environments

People

Things

Experiences

Write your answers to the prompts on the following pages.

Inspiring Environments

Personally or professionally, what is an environment where you had a **great idea or realization**? *At your desk, on a vacation, at a conference….* Try to be specific about the location.

_____

_____

_____

_____

_____

What do you remember most in terms of qualities of this environment? How did you feel? What aspect do you remember most?

_____

_____

_____

_____

_____

_____

Inspiration

Inspiring People

Who is a person that has inspired or continues to inspire you? Who is someone that encouraged you or gave you the confidence to move forward? *This could be a mentor, a teacher, an influencer, a celebrity, a parent...*

_____

_____

_____

_____

_____

What did they do, specifically, and how did it change your perspective or your actions?

_____

_____

_____

_____

_____

Sources of Inspiration

Do you read any specific websites, blogs, books, magazines, or journals that inspire you? What are sources of Inspiration that give you ideas and motivation? What do you read, listen to, or watch not because you have to but because you want to?

_____

_____

_____

_____

_____

What about these sources inspires you? Are they visually inspiring? Are they emotionally resonant or positive? Do the concepts challenge you to think in new ways? How have they changed your actions or perspective?

_____

_____

_____

_____

_____

Inspiration

Inspirational Experiences

What experiences have inspired you? What experiences have given you fresh energy, ideas, or motivation? *This could be something you do regularly or a one-time experience you had...*

_____

_____

_____

_____

_____

What about the experience was inspiring? How did it change your perspective, motivate you, or prompt you to expand your perception of your potential?

_____

_____

_____

_____

Exercise 2: Expand Your Sources

Since Inspiration is literally "the act of drawing in", we must find sources of Inspiration to draw in new ideas and energy. Inspiration helps us get un-stuck! Some ways to seek and find new sources of Inspiration are below. After browsing the sources below, you'll make a plan for how to move forward in expanding your sources of Inspiration this month.

New Sources of Inspiration

◆ Community (*often free*): look for opportunities in your community to attend events that interest you. Most towns or cities have many industry-related or interest-related groups.

◆ Books *(low cost, or free from a library)*: A favorite, of course! Books are a great way to learn from other people and to learn new things at your own speed and on your own time. Visit my website for recommendations or ask friends and co-workers.

◆ Conferences: Conferences are a good way to learn, network, and gain ideas from others working in your field and with similar interests. Ask peers or your leader for recommendations.

◆ Ted Talks (*free*): Visit ted.com and search for topics or influencers that interest you. The trending and all-time best videos are a good place to start watching. These talks are short so they are great for starting your day, taking a short break at work, or to watch alone or with your team during lunch.

Inspiration

New Sources of Inspiration

◆ Podcasts (*free with Internet*): search podcasts for interesting topics and influencers. They are a really great resource to listen to while exercising or taking a break!

◆ Courses or Workshops (*some free*): Obviously attending courses and workshops sparks ideas and new connections.

◆ Nature (*often free*): Our breath is fuller in nature and nature serves as Inspiration for how we can work more mindfully. Take a walk in nature for a break and return to work refreshed.

◆ Travel: Oh, travel, need I say more? Travel expands our knowledge and opens our mind to new ideas and possibility. It changes our perspective. Whether traveling for holiday or on a work or personal-related mission, travel helps us to changeup our day-to-day routine and return with new energy, knowledge, ideas and perspective.

◆ Museums (*often free*): Museums are fun as a team event or to go alone to learn and think. They are usually very peaceful (if a more sophisticated museum), energizing, and rich with ideas.

◆ Journals and Publications (*some free*): Though we do most of our reading (or scrolling) on the Internet these days, journals and magazines are still my favorite way to read news and find ideas.

New Sources of Inspiration

◆ Movies and TV(*often free, with Internet*): Another favorite. Entertainment is healing, energizing, and shifts our perspective. TV shows that feature challenge, relationships, and trajectories are inspiring. I think we all have some movies that have inspired us along our path. Find movies that resonate! It's always helpful to use quotes and metaphors from well-known movies with your team.

◆ Your leader, other leaders in your organization (*free*): Of course, have lunch or coffee to meet with your leader or leaders in your organization that inspire you. They'll most likely be flattered and happy to connect.

◆ Friends (*the most amazing free source*): My **most** favorite! Friends are inspiring. Find friends in your organization on your team or from different areas of the organization to celebrate wins with, learn from, and (importantly) vent to and support each other. You'll be inspired by each others' stories and paths.

Inspiration

Response and Planning

From my sources of Inspiration listed or your own ideas, what is one new source of Inspiration you can try out this month?

_____

_____

Why do you feel this experience or source will inspire you?

_____

_____

What do you need to do to plan it? What steps do you need to take? Is anything stopping you?

_____

_____

Can you plan a date to do it? When - now? What date?

_____

Can you commit? Can you put aside the time?

_____

Exercise 3: Team Inspiration

This is a more structured exercise for cultivating Inspiration that is Vision-related! Try planning some of these inspirational activities with your team. You'll be surprised at how you return to work with new energy, ideas, and motivation. Some team activities that spark Inspiration and cultivate connection are below.

Source 1: Time away from the office as a team

There are many things you can do as a team to get out of the office to connect with each other and gain Inspiration. It's worth the time.

A fun and easy activity is to plan a team lunch. Pick your favorite lunch spot near the office and put lunch with your team on the calendar. You should all drive together if possible and make sure your organization will cover the bill. Context Immersion trips also count as Inspiration adventures.

Source 2: Readings and Discussion

Chose a recent article from an industry-related website or magazine and have the team read it as preparation for a team meeting. Discuss the article together. This is a way to cultivate and gauge interest in the content of the work and also to learn more about your team members. What do they find interesting? Let them know it's not a test but a team activity. Maybe even have them choose a favorite quote or takeaway from the article to bring to the meeting to share.

Inspiration

Source 3: Puzzle!

My favorite activity with my team at the office was when I brought a 1008-piece jigsaw puzzle. I kept it on a large table in my office and we worked on it as a team for about a month, a little each day or a few times per week. Team members would come in the office when they wanted a few minutes for a break from their work. Puzzles are great for relieving anxiety, for team bonding, for constructive rest, and for problem solving.

Source 4: Exercises 1 and 2 with your Team

For more ideas and to gauge what inspires your team, do Exercises 1 and 2 with your team. Give them the Exercise 1 prompts and Exercises 2 ideas for expansion to do on their own and share as a team.

Awake Tip 6

Encourage Constructive Rest

When your team feels their energy is waning (or you do), periodic breaks prevent burnout and improve productivity. Many leaders set strict rules and discourage team members from taking breaks. However, breaks like sitting for a few minutes when customers are not in the store or walking outside between tasks to get out of the office stimulate fresh energy, more positive interactions, and enhance productivity. I call this kind of break *from work during work* Constructive Rest. It's rest that fuels the work. It's not engaging in political conversations or watching videos but rest that refuels and reinvigorates.

Different people require different amounts and types of Constructive Rest. It doesn't mean they're lazy or taking advantage, unless you feel that is the intention. In that case, bring it up during a one-on-one meeting, but always intend to support their best work and foster a relationship of trust. We often come up with the best ideas for how to solve challenges or unresolved issues after returning from a walk alone, taking a few deep breaths, enjoying a coffee, or having a quick conversation with a colleague. I found that when I encouraged Constructive Rest, team members showed up to meetings with energy and a positive attitude.

When you have a week with a lot of work demands or a big project meeting, allow and encourage sufficient Constructive Rest for your team and yourself. Don't deprive yourself or postpone it!

Inspiration gives you and your team members new ideas, as well as motivation for shaping and executing your Vision.

7
Freedom

noun;

the absence of necessity, coercion, or constraint in choice or action

liberation from restraint or from the power of another

unrestricted use

Freedom

What is Freedom?

Freedom is the ability to choose **where to place your awareness** and **how to spend your time**. When you feel a sense of Freedom, you feel as though you are energetic, connected, and engaged in something you want to focus on and work on. The work feels full of healthy challenge. Do you feel like you have a sense of Freedom in your work and life right now?

Freedom involves taking initiative. This is why Freedom is the final and most advanced vital. Taking ownership of your attention and time is the first step in shaping the world versus following. Most people get in their own way of Freedom because they do not spend the time to find their version of Freedom in action.

Where does Freedom come from?

When you are a leader within an organization, Freedom comes from you, your leader, and the top-level leadership. Many leaders provide too little Freedom for themselves and their team members. This is usually because they weren't or aren't given Freedom in their own work or life. Practices that are Freedom blockers include micromanaging and dictator-like behavior. A lack of Freedom feels limiting or stifling.

Working in an organization is often the best way to start digging into what you like and don't like, and what freedom ultimately means for you. As you learn what your interests are, you learn what Freedom in action is for you. You first have to desire Freedom and take initiative of your attention and time. You have already done this by working through the guidebook, starting with Vision! Remember that the right amount of Freedom versus Structure differs from person to person, and it changes over time. Some people like a lot of direction at work so that they can focus on life outside of work. More creative leaders and team members usually desire and demand more Freedom.

Why is Freedom a leadership vital?

First and foremost, Freedom gives your leadership authenticity. Practicing Freedom makes you YOU. Practicing discernment is the first step in assuming the role of a leader; shaping your Team Vision and your larger Vision for your career and your life. All the other vitals prepare you to do exactly this.

Freedom is also related to health and happiness. When you hold yourself back from your desires in terms of how to spend your time and where to place your attention, it eventually results in mental and physical health problems.

Finally, a sense of Freedom fuels great work toward the Vision. When you feel a sense of Freedom, you take ownership of your work and take genuine interest in seeing it through successfully. Team members are happiest when they have a sense of Freedom balanced with guidance and direction from a trusted leader. They are able to learn about their strengths and interests while developing new skills and connections.

In the Freedom exercises, you'll explore the questions: *What is my Freedom in action? What is my ideal balance of Structure and Freedom? How can I provide a better balance of Structure and Freedom for my team members?* You'll work on finding your Freedom and ways to give your team members Freedom that fuels their authenticity and best work toward the Vision.

Freedom

Freedom Exercises

The purpose of the Freedom exercises is to find your Freedom in action and serve as a guide in helping your team to do the same.

In the first exercise, you'll learn my favorite way of kick-starting your practice of Freedom. In the second exercise, you'll learn how to give your team members a sense of Freedom balanced with guidance. Finally, you'll explore how to find your Freedom in action. Let's begin!

Exercise 1: Daily Pages

Exercise 2: Team Round Table Presentations

Exercise 3: Freedom in Action

Supplies

✎ Pencil or pen
✎ Notebook

Freedom

Exercise 1: Daily Pages

The way to begin practicing your Freedom and building your authenticity is to develop your own voice, explore your dreams and desires, and reflect on your progress. This exercise is adapted from Julia Cameron's book, *The Artist's Way*.

Free writing is a simple method of intentionally placing your attention and time where you want and need to. This practice of daily free writing changed my leadership style for the better and changed my life. I worked with more intention and confidence. When you do daily writing, your team will feel that you are more grounded, prepared, and confident each day when you show up to work.

Each morning, spend at least 20 minutes free writing. You can write in a journal or on your laptop. My favorite time to write is first thing in the morning when my mind is clear and fresh. I love writing in the morning because the world is quiet and I can reflect on the previous day from a rational, energized place and think about how I want to move forward today. Whether you give yourself a morning pep talk, write about what happened the day before, or write about how this guide is working for you, you'll begin to develop your own voice. You will hone in on who you are and what is important to you.

As you write, try to write in complete sentences. Don't try too hard - the writing should be casual and reflect your voice. No one needs to see it or know about it. I believe it takes at least 20 minutes to one hour to really dig in and start to get to the deeper realizations. Find a quiet space, alone (no TV blasting or scanning the newspaper as you write) and enjoy.

I have provided some prompts on the following page. Pick one or more of my prompts that interest you or start free writing to your own prompt.

Writing Prompts

◆ What has been the most satisfying milestone of your work this past year?

◆ What satisfying progress did you make in your work or life this past month?

◆ Did anything unexpected or challenging happen this past month? How did you work through it?

◆ What new experiences have you had or what new people have you met lately that inspired or motivated you?

◆ What are the very unique abilities you have?

◆ What aspects of your personality make you uniquely YOU?

◆ What are you looking forward to most this month or this year? Why?

◆ What are you not looking forward to this month or this year? What would you eliminate from your schedule this year if you could? Why?

◆ What dreams do you have that you have put aside? Why?

◆ Is the Mission and Vision for your team clear? Why or why not?

◆ How are you living your leadership intentions? How are you living your life intentions?

Freedom

Exercise 2: Round Table Presentations

This exercise is an opportunity for your team members to identify what interests them most about their work or the organization. Identifying interests and facilitating discussion is not only a key leadership skill but also a way of cultivating authenticity and Freedom. Team members will develop curiosity and confidence you will gain more knowledge about what truly interests them.

The Exercise

Kick off the exercise by asking your team members to make a short presentation about something they're currently working on. You can suggest a project they're working on from the Vision Map or give them a new project or topic that you come up with together. The project or assignment should be related to the Team Vision.

Giving Guidance

Use this opportunity to mentor your team members. In your one-on-one meetings, discuss and review progress. Note what team members are interested in so you can keep their work engaging.

Asking your team members to put together a presentation may not sound like Freedom. It may seem as though you're giving them something else to do. This is the guidance aspect - the Structure. However, this initial prompt and guidance provides an opportunity for team members to practice reflection about what truly interests them, what they're curious about, and choose what topic or area to place their attention on. They may need to brainstorm with you. It's also an opportunity to learn how to lead a project, express interests, and show progress through their own perspective and voice.

Presentations

The presentation should be interesting and engaging for the team. They should discuss what they found challenging or interesting about the project or topic, and prompt the team for feedback. Team members love knowing what other team members are working on and exchanging ideas. Encourage each team member, including yourself, to ask at least one question at the end of the presentation. Practice giving a balance of positive and constructive feedback.

Exercise 3: Freedom in Action

In this final exercise, you will continue to explore what Freedom is for you in action. It will feel weird to write answers to these prompts at first, but this is how to practice your Freedom, develop independence, and make authentic progress. This exercise can also be used for taking insights from your Daily Pages into action.

Prompts for Freedom in Action

If you could spend a day doing any activity, what would you choose to do? What do you crave?

_____

_____

_____

_____

If you could take any course or training to learn something new, what topic would you choose to learn more about? What are you curious about?

_____

_____

_____

_____

Does your current work and Team Vision spark your interest? Why or why not?

_____

_____

_____

_____

_____

_____

How does your current organization's mission in action align with your own values? How does it differ from or conflict with your values?

_____

_____

_____

_____

_____

_____

Freedom

Do feel that you currently have a sense of Freedom at work and in your life? Why or why not?

_____

_____

_____

_____

_____

_____

What changes could you make this week to incorporate more Freedom in action into your work and life?

_____

_____

_____

_____

_____

_____

Awake Tip 7

Balance Structure and Freedom

At work, team members need to be given a balance of guidance and creative Freedom to practice using their own discernment and find their authentic way of working and leading. Here are three suggestions for finding the right balance of Structure and Freedom that works for your team members and for you.

First, encourage learning whenever possible by giving responsibility. It takes courage and trust on the part of the leader to hand over responsibility and to allow learning to happen. If team members make mistakes, allow them to have the experience of making and owning a mistake. If they never fall down, they'll never understand the implications and how to recover. Always step back and consider it a learning investment when something doesn't go as planned. Reflect on it with your team members to learn for next time. Allowing team members to try new things and to learn is a form of Freedom, rather than being micromanaged. Also, making team members more independent always helps when you're on vacation! It helps your Freedom, too.

Secondly, don't over-structure schedules and enforce limitations that don't fuel each individual's best work. There is not a one-size-fits-all schedule. Agree to align at a high level for team functionality but allow maximum flexibility in work time and place that fuels the Vision. If team members want to work 12-hour days, cool. However, don't make it an expected team practice or a norm. As long as the collective team Vision is moving forward, breathe. Maybe even talk to your leader about loosening some of the restricting policies. The enforced structure should fuel the Vision and team

Awake Tip 7

Balance Structure and Freedom

members should understand why. If you don't agree with a rule or your organization's Structure, try following it for a while to give it a chance and then ask about it respectfully to understand the policy and its value. Maybe your leader will be able to answer your doubt or change the rule. Sometimes you don't have to leave an organization to find more Freedom if you speak up and voice things that would both improve your Freedom and the organization's Vision.

Finally, encourage your team to live dynamically outside of work and place time and attention on a variety of things that interest them. They'll bring back great ideas, come into work refreshed and with positives vibes. If they don't, they may soon find this Vision is not for them and they belong somewhere else that aligns more with their Freedom.

When you find a sense of Freedom, things unfold naturally and the work is accomplished with more ease an enthusiasm. Let the wind and waves take you where they will. Allow yourself to live dynamically outside of your work. Then, return to the Vision.

Freedom is the ability to choose where to place your awareness and how to spend your time.

Continuing the Practice

Continuing the Practice

You have made one round up the staircase. Congratulations! Where to now? Do we go right back to the Vision and do it again? Not so fast. We have done all of this work to understand how you work toward your current Team Vision. Now it's time to put what we have observed and planned into action. Now it's time for practice and iteration.

Practice takes a few different forms. It may seem like there are so many exercises to start doing. Start by focusing on Vision, Support, and Structure. These three sections are the foundation of the system. First and foremost, work your current Vision Map tasks and activities. Execute the Vision Map by sticking to your activities and tasks as planned on your map. Meet with your team weekly to align on the Vision Map together. Once you have your Vision Map in action and have gathered the Support you need, then identify the exercises in the following sections that will best serve your team. Try them gradually, one by one. I especially suggest you do Daily Pages yourself and plan team Context Immersions if you're looking for a place to begin.

Ultimately, this system is a blueprint for you to use and to make your own. You know best which exercises will benefit your team and yourself at any given period in time. You may at times go back to a specific section. You may go back to a specific, favorite exercise over and over again. You may even develop your own variations of the exercises or your own original exercises.

There is not a specification for how often you should update your Role Map or Vision Map and work through the vitals again. I would suggest updating your Role Map and Vision Map at least every three months to refresh and realign. However, you could revisit and revamp your maps every month or every week. It's fun to look back at past iterations of the Vision Map with your team and see how tasks have changed and how many projects and objectives have been accomplished.

Gather experience and insights to refine and improve as you continue up the spiral staircase.

◆　◆　◆

Wrap-Up Exercise

Today's Date: _____

The vital that is most relevant to focus on with my team this month:

_____

Three exercises I'm going to do with my team this month:

_____

_____

The vital that resonated with me as most relevant for me personally:

_____

One (or more) exercise I'm going to do myself this month:

_____

Essential Questions and Answers

Here are answers to a few favorite frequently asked questions.

Why would someone aspire to be a leader?

Whether you are a leader of a team, or a leader of purely your work and life, you'll find taking responsibility and ownership to move forward is satisfying and inspiring. Leading prompts you to practice discernment, develop a point of view, and gain deeper awareness about yourself and the world. As you lead your team members, you'll see and embrace how each individual and their path is similar and different from your own. Leading someone or leading a team offers the opportunity to more deeply connect with and learn from other people.

Leading a team is inspiring because teams have the capability to accomplish things that would not be possible to do alone. Each person's contributions are essential but the collective makes the larger Vision possible. There's a sense of interdependence that you can only experience when you work with a dedicated team.

You can still be a leader of your work and your life as a team member or a solo worker without any people to formally lead. Leadership is a development and growth position, whether that means developing a business, developing a team, or developing an outcome or result of a project.

What is success as a leader?

To be a successful leader, you must take specific actions that guide the Vision and the team forward. There are many leadership books that provide principles, qualities, attributes, and examples of "successful" leadership. All of these books are important but they seldom give guidance for **how** - *in action* - you can show up to work and be successful. You can use ideas from stories you read and apply them to certain decisions but how that leader approached it may not be right for you, in your specific situation.

Before you know what is right or successful, you must start experiencing and studying what is right for you and for your team, not theoretically but in actuality. This system gives you guidance for how to start leading and experiencing today, no matter what work or team you lead. Through the experience and observation, you'll learn what success is for you and your team.

For now, to be successful, I ask that you try the system and work through the guidebook to the end. The only way is through experience. There is no magical advice or perfect example of what leadership success is for you. Everyone has a different version of success and that is what you will find through using the system: your version of success as a leader.

You must believe that you have the ability and commit to endlessly learning. You must have a strong desire to take responsibility and ownership of a vision to improve and develop it. You must be curious and enthusiastic about the world and about people. Specific actions and positive beliefs about yourself and the world will make you successful. So, the best place to start to become a successful leader is to practice being a leader of your own work, life, and team.

What are <u>qualities</u> of a successful leader?

Many aspiring leaders also ask what qualities they need to have in order to be a successful leader. There is no set of qualities that make a perfect leader. By trying to identify if you have certain natural leadership qualities, you're not allowing yourself to develop your authenticity and potential as a leader. The right qualities depend on the person and the situation.

The right leadership qualities for you are developed through specific actions in practice. This is why you must start with the actions that work to align and progress with your team. You will cultivate your essential leadership qualities by using this system and taking the actions that work, in a way that works, for your team.

While I will not mention specific qualities, here is a review of some of the attributes and abilities Awake leaders develop through using the system. From your round up the staircase, you may now see how these qualities emerging.

An Awake leader is enthusiastic about change and people. An Awake leader responds to changes and reaches objectives efficiently and creatively with the team. He or she is clear on the team Vision and maximizes the strengths of the team. An Awake leader displays dedication, driven by curiosity. He or she has a balance of hard and soft skills. An Awake leader is authentically inspirational and influential. He or she enjoys learning, analyzing, and synthesizing. An Awake leader can zoom in to understand detail and zoom out to see the big picture impacts. He or she generates ideas for how to evolve, sustainably solve problems, and supports change and growth in the company through efficient execution. An Awake leader walks the walk and leads by example. An Awake leader cultivates enthusiasm, curiosity, and a culture of collaboration and follow through. An Awake leader has a mindful method to their madness.

As an Awake leader, you will develop the courage to ask questions and give your point of view instead of following and obeying without resolving doubts. You will be a healthy skeptic that will not stop until you have done all you can to gain clarity. You will start to appreciate how clarity and the right amount of Structure provide a foundation for Freedom.

You will develop a positive, solution-centric mindset. You may also find yourself striving to develop creative solutions that work in the interest of the whole. This is often more challenging than just building a wall to block out problems or claiming and winner and a loser. There are always trade-offs, but Awake leaders find solutions that maximize the good for everyone involved.

You will find that you lead with the intentions of enjoying your experience day-to-day and cultivating genuine connections with others. Intentions of achievement based on money alone, labels, and pride may start to fall away.

Exciting? I hope so!

What about pushback or resistance from others?

Now that you have read this book, you may find that you have become very intentional and mindful of your actions as a leader. You may feel more sensitive, aware, and curious about the actions other individuals take. How will you deal with leaders, peers, and team members (or people in your life in general) that have not studied this system? How will you collaborate with people who do not have clear intentions of leading with a balance of Structure and Freedom? How will you deal with leaders that don't value clarity and creativity? How will you deal with others that don't strive to align and motivate their team? I have found that we all have these intentions deep down, however, they get buried under things like fear, conditioning, and distraction. Don't let others or the overwhelming state of the situation discourage you from moving forward with clarity, creativity, and authenticity.

Try out these approaches to resistance in the field:

Lead by Example and Communicate: Don't allow others to affect your approach. This is easier said than done when your leader, peers, or team members are resistant, closed-minded, or bad communicators. These individuals need to gradually awaken and that is what Awake leaders help others to do kindly, lovingly, and persistently. We primarily do this by using the system ourselves and leading by example, but also by giving honest feedback to others directly. To use this system, the only approval you need is your own. When you use the system to gain clarity about what you are doing and why, truly, you gain courage to express that to others. If you find that your leader or organization is stopping you from using the system, have a candid, honest conversation to align on intentions or go somewhere where you can lead authentically and lead by example. Don't wait too long.

Teach: Use my examples as well as the exercises you have practiced to teach your team and other leaders how to use the system. Some days you may need to reflect to determine which vitals are off and which exercises to use. You are fortunate to have a live environment to practice using and teaching the system in action. Teaching will help you to keep your dedication to your own leadership system and practice, too.

Be patient and persistent: Some days you may need to take rest and time alone to reflect. As you practice more and more, it will become easier to navigate decisions and choose actions. Some days you may feel resistance. Be patient and persistent. You'll gain confidence. Others will respect you and trust you.

Continue to use the system to experience, observe, and reflect. Missing any of these three actions in sequence may cause you to find yourself wandering down the wrong path. This is okay and it happens. Just know it takes time to get back on track and reconnect to your true intentions, practices, and qualities.

Share: You can share this book with your friends, family, and co-workers. If your organization has a leadership program or development program, this book is a good resource to add to it.

How do you know if the system is working?

Do you feel like you are clear about your Vision? Do you feel that you are more efficiently and enthusiastically accomplishing your objectives and overall mission with your team? Are you progressing collectively and individually? Are you happier? Is your team happier?

If your answers to these questions is **Yes**, then it's working!

By practicing the Awake Leadership system to align and motivate your team toward your collective and individual objectives, you will lead by example and pass these practices and positive vibes onto others. You will enjoy the quest for finding that sweet balance of Structure and Freedom that works for each unique individual and team. In turn, you will find it for yourself, in your work and your life. If you want your career and your future team, organization, and the world to sustain and succeed authentically, Awake Leadership is crucial. Patience, persistence, and positivity are key.

Congratulations on completing your round up the staircase and I wish you great happiness and success as you continue on your journey.

◆　◆　◆

Author's Notes

The Pace

A Guide for Working through Awake Leadership

The sample schedule below gives you some guidance for how
to work through the book.

Vision Exercises	→ Week 1
Support Exercises	→ Week 2
Structure Exercises	→ Week 3
Reflect, Practice, Observe	→ Week 4
Tools Exercises	→ Week 5
Reflect, Practice, Observe	→ Week 6
Context Exercises	→ Week 7
Reflect, Practice, Observe	→ Week 8
Inspiration Exercises	→ Week 9
Reflect, Practice, Observe	→ Week 10
Freedom Exercises	→ Week 11
Reflect, Practice, Observe	→ Weeks 12-16
Return to Vision Plan	→ Week 17

Note: I did not put this schedule in the Introduction because
every leader has their own pace to work through the book. Feel
free to move through it at the pace you like and that is realistic
for you to get the most out of it and put the exercises into
practice. The sample schedule above gives you some guidance,
from my experience, of how to work through the guide without
feeling overwhelmed and giving up. You will onboard, through
sections 1-3, in your first month and you'll be through the guide
within your first quarter (first three months).

The Chakra System

The Awake Leadership system is inspired by the Chakra system, an ancient system of yoga. The Chakra system originated in India over four thousand years ago. Many people in the United States and western society have heard of the Chakra system since yoga has grown as an industry and the influence has spread. My appreciation of the Chakra system has deepened throughout my ten plus years of practicing and teaching yoga.

The Chakra system is a very useful system for understanding the universal vitals of human life on a physical and conscious level. Just like the Awake Leadership system, the Chakra system serves as a system for understanding where we have blind spots or imbalances that create obstacles or cause pain.

According to the Chakra system, humans have seven centers in our body that energy flows through. The word *Chakra* literally translates as *wheel* or *disk,* since they represent spinning wheels of energy. Each Chakra relates to a different point in the body as well as an aspect of human consciousness. When all the vitals are healthy and balanced, physical and conscious energy freely flows throughout the body. Underdeveloped or blocked energy centers can lead to illnesses or imbalances. In the traditional system, an imbalance also often means there is a blockage between our mundane physical and our spiritual lives.

Just as the way to unblock or balance your leadership style is by practicing the exercises in the Awake Leadership system, the way to unblock or balance out your Chakras is by practicing yoga.

If you would like to learn more about the Chakra system, I highly recommend reading *Eastern Mind, Western Body* by Anodea Judith. This book is not only an excellent book for learning more about the Chakra system but one of my most treasured books for personal development.

The Chakra System

Crown Chakra
Cognition

Brow Chakra
Intuition

Throat Chakra
Communication

Heart Chakra
Love

Solar Plexus Chakra
Power

Abdomen Chakra
Sexuality

Base of Spine Chakra
Survival

Role Map Template

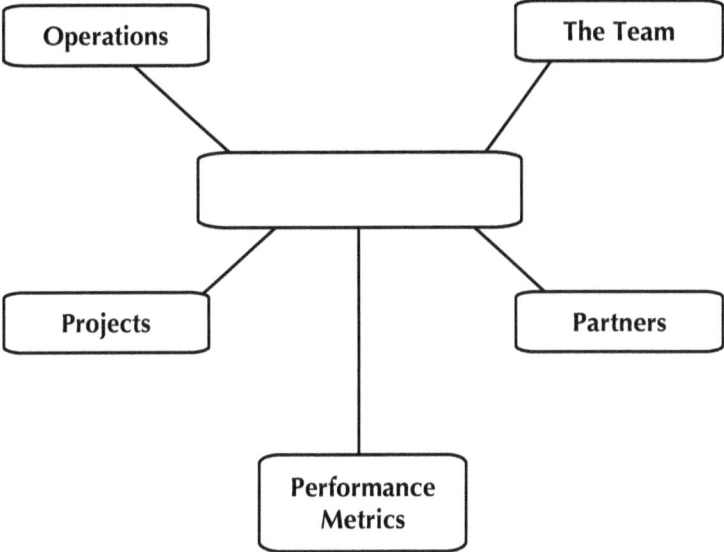

Operations

The Team

[central box — blank]

Projects

Partners

Performance
Metrics

Vision Map Template

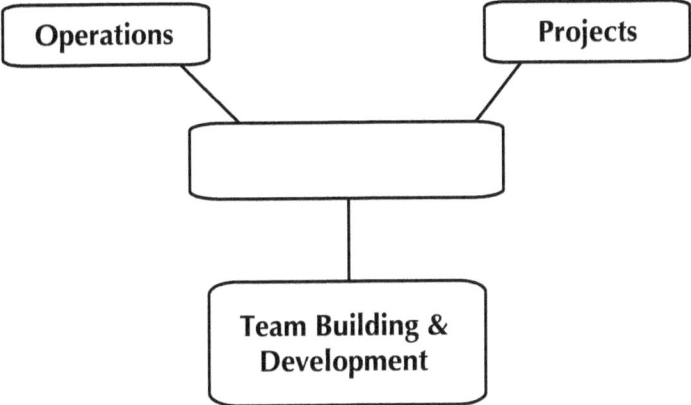

```
┌──────────────────┐                    ┌──────────────────┐
│   Operations     │                    │    Projects      │
└──────────────────┘                    └──────────────────┘
          \                                    /
           \                                  /
            ┌──────────────────────────────┐
            │                              │
            └──────────────────────────────┘
                          │
                          │
                ┌──────────────────────┐
                │  Team Building &     │
                │    Development       │
                └──────────────────────┘
```

AN 8

Thank You Notes

Thanks to my many leaders and peers for giving me the opportunity to be a leader and for incredible experience, understanding, and knowledge.

Thanks to the rising leaders that continue to ask questions and inspire each other as we work together and strive to be the best we can be.

Thanks to all of my teachers and community for support and encouragement. I am beyond grateful for my teachers and the community for reminding me to take care of myself and show up, one day at a time, to dig deep, see clearly, and be the change I want to see in the world.

Thanks to the big thinkers, writers, artists, and creatives for sharing your powerful ideas and work. Thank you for your loving push, even from afar, through your words and works, to tune in and take a risk.

Thanks to my editors, for helping me to share my ideas clearly.

Last and surely not least, many thanks to my family members and friends, for supporting me and giving me enthusiastic feedback and positive vibes along the way.

About Hilary

Hilary Jane Grosskopf is a leadership guide, strategist, and writer. Her writing is inspired by her experience as a leader in a variety of organizations and her study of systems. As Founder of Awake Leadership Solutions, she helps leaders to develop strong leadership skills, build the teams of their dreams, and achieve bold objectives.

awakeleadershipsolutions.com

Also by Hilary

Awake Ethics
A system for aligning your actions with your core intentions.

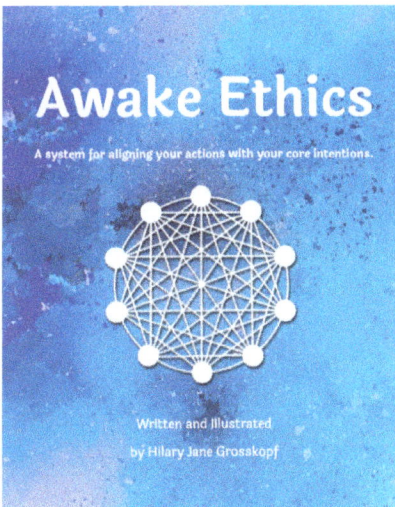

Awake Ethics illustrates how a system of ten ethical principles, when put into practice, enable human-centered progress. In order to successfully lead a team or modern organization, leaders must learn to cultivate both peace and progress. Through stories from the field, prompts, and interactive exercises, learn how to align your actions with your intentions for connection, creativity, and satisfying progress.

Available on Amazon.com.

Learn more at awakeleadershipsolutions.com.

Awake Leadership

www.ingramcontent.com/pod-product-compliance
Lightning Source LLC
Chambersburg PA
CBHW050106220326

41598CB00043B/7397